THE ORIGIN AND NAMING OF BRANFORD'S STREETS

THE ORIGIN & NAMING OF
Branford's Streets

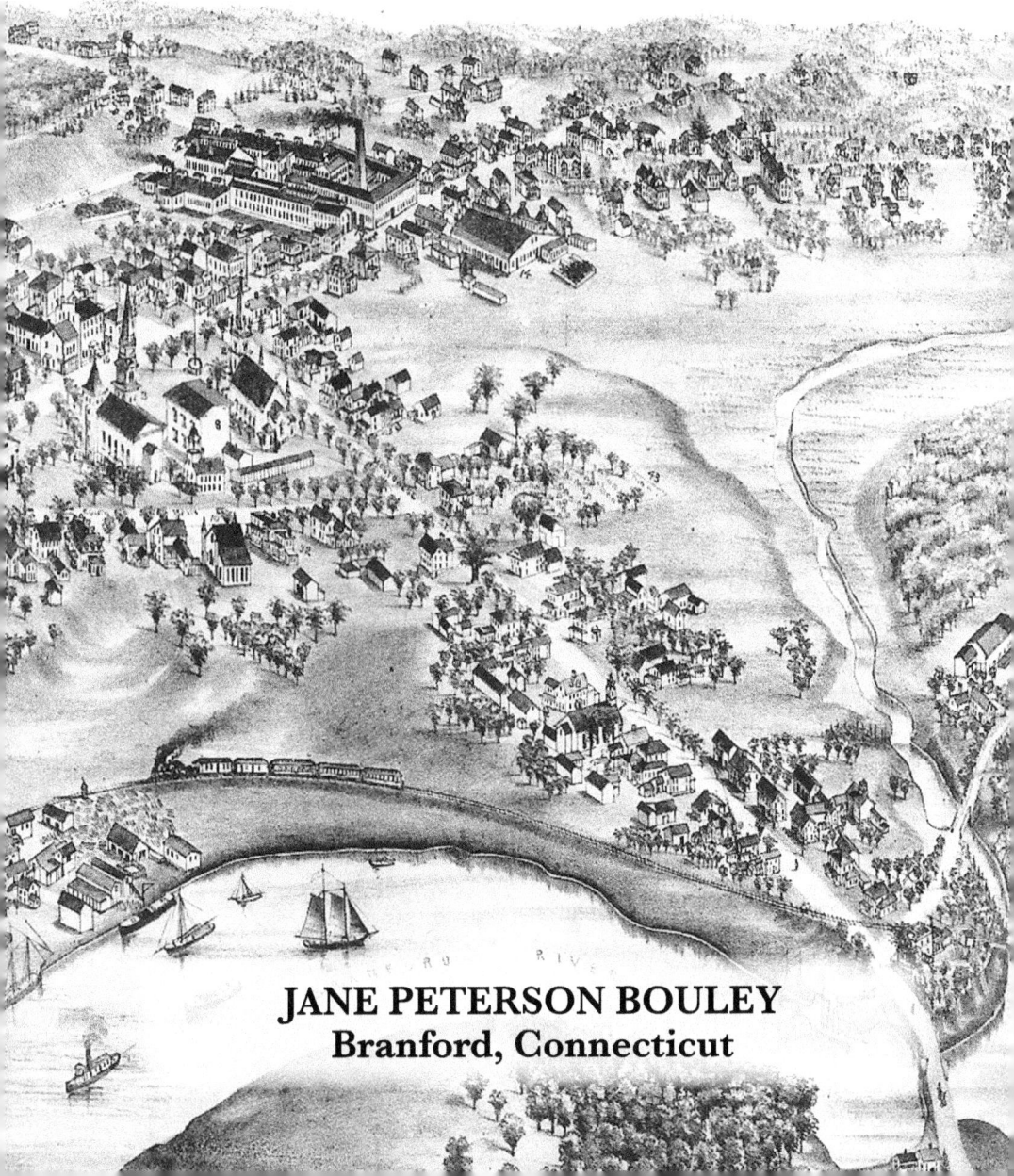

JANE PETERSON BOULEY
Branford, Connecticut

THE ORIGIN AND NAMING OF BRANFORD'S STREETS
Copyright ©2018, Jane Peterson Bouley

All rights reserved. No part of this book may be used or reproduced by any means, graphic, electronic, or mechanical, including photocopying, recording, taping or by any information storage retrieval system without the written permission of the publisher except in the case of brief quotations embodied in critical articles and reviews.

Because of the dynamic nature of the Internet, any web addresses or links contained in this book may have changed since publication and may no longer be valid. The views expressed in this work are solely those of the author and do not necessarily reflect the views of the publisher, and the publisher hereby disclaims any responsibility for them.

All photos, unless otherwise noted in the text, are used with permission from the Branford Historical Society.

Author photo by Bill O'Brien, Branford, Connecticut
Book design by Words by Jen, Jennifer A. Payne

ISBN: 978-0-692-24891-1

Printed in the United States of America

TABLE OF CONTENTS

Introduction	vii
About the Streets	1
Repositories & Resources	7
The Streets, Alphabetical	15
Appendix	209
Streets Named for People or Families	211
Streets Named for Nature	213
Streets Named for Places or Objects	214
Endnotes	215
Bibliography	236
About the Author	238

Western end of Linden Avenue looking east showing The Ace, a summer store.

INTRODUCTION

The development of the streets in Branford center and its neighborhoods bear testament to the town's history. Street names were derived from nature, families, and sometimes appear to be arbitrary. A close examination of the origin of various streets and the buildings along them follows Branford's history through the colonial period, as an 18th century farming community, during the industrial revolution bringing an influx of European immigrants in the 19th and 20th centuries, and finally as a suburban community after World War II.

This book is the culmination of several decades of research using many different resources.[1] No one book, map, or repository provides a complete list or history of Branford's streets. Until 1958, there were many streets in town bearing the same name. For example, there was a Main Street in Branford center, Stony Creek, and Short Beach in addition to South Main Street, East Main Street, West Main Street, and the newer North Main Street. Many street names were changed at that time mandated by the U. S. Post Office to simplify postal delivery.

Some streets were known by different names during the same time-period, one used officially and the other used locally by the residents. Or, the name changed several times over decades or centuries, especially colonial roads. Early deeds often did not name the road, simply calling it "the highway." Also making research more difficult regarding specific buildings is the use of house numbers. Numbers were not used in many neighborhoods until 1960[2] when the use of house numbers was mandated by the U. S. Postal Service. In Branford center, for reasons now unknown, building numbers and sections of street names were changed. The James Blackstone Memorial Library at 758 Main Street was 134 Main Street. The Harrison House at 124 Main Street, home of the Branford Historical Society, was 112 West Main Street.

The streets in the book are listed alphabetically and included is the date or approximate date of origin, neighborhood, cross street, map references, and a brief history. Streets built after 1980 are not included, the naming of which tend to not have any historical significance.

The Naming and Origin of Branford's Streets is patterned after Doris B. Townshend's book *The Streets of East Haven*, published in 1992.

> Jane P. Bouley
> Branford, Connecticut
> 2018

ABOUT THE STREETS

The English settlers used Indian paths to construct their roads and built new streets in Branford center. Many of these early streets are still in use today such as Montowese Street, Cherry Hill Road, Main Street, and Brushy Plain Road. Most roadways were built or sanctioned by the town and approved at a Town Meeting. It was not until 1926 that the Selectmen determined that no road could be built using town money and the owners of the land had to build the street at their own expense. The building of the new street would be supervised by and built under town specifications such as grade and sidewalks. When the street was finished, the town would accept the road upon approval of the Board of Selectmen and a vote at the Town Meeting.[3] It was not until the 20th century that large developments were built. Some streets remained private. Today building and accepting a street is much the same; specifications by the Engineering Department, approval by the Representative Town

Meeting (which replaced the centuries old Town Meeting in 1959) and by the Board of Selectmen.[4]

Proving that a street was accepted as a town road is often not easy. The building of a street may appear in a Town Meeting report, but a deed was never entered into the land records. In the late 19th and early 20th centuries, a survey of a new street or reconfiguration of an existing street was mandated by the Selectmen with the survey completed by a surveyor or engineer. Terminology can be confusing. The surveys are titled "survey and layout of a new road in…." Sometimes it is not a new road but a regrading or widening of an existing road. The survey was accepted at the Town Meeting and a deed placed in the land records. This only constitutes accepting the survey, not accepting it as a town road. Some roads never made it past the survey stage. Even during the 20th century, the Representative Town Meeting (RTM) may have voted to accept a street and forward it to the Board of Selectmen. Sometimes it never appeared on the Selectmen's agenda or in the Selectmen meeting minutes.

The town hired men from the neighborhoods to widen and clear town roads. This group is widening Damascus Road in 1934. Photo by Charles A. Blackstone.

About the Streets

Another difficulty is the description of the street and correlating it to today's boundaries. Deeds refer to trees or rock features as boundaries. Often roads are referred to as "the highway or shore road." Descriptions of roads in deeds or official records can read as follows: A piece of highway 75 rods from the dwelling of Chauncey Rogers known as Gravel Knoll northeasterly by the highway, westerly by a ledge of rocks to a heap of stones on said ledge, southerly by a cluster of rocks adjoining the peach nursery, thence 50 feet to said highway. Even the town sometimes used names for streets that were not official; for example, a 1918 Town Report lists repairs on Higley Street. There is no other document or map listing Higley Street. In Short Beach "all roads in Short Beach which are used or have been used by the public" were accepted as town roads in 1930. The streets were not listed. Since the exact boundary of Short Beach is not defined, does it include streets along Alps Road or Double Beach? Roads or portions of roads were abandoned, the descriptions of which are equally difficult to ascertain.

Maps are an essential part of researching streets. Maps for Branford Center tend to be quite detailed but streets in the summer neighborhoods such as Short Beach and Indian Neck often lack detail. Some of the streets in these neighborhoods do not appear on maps until the mid-20th century.

Branford's roadways were originally dirt and covered with a variety of materials such as stone, oyster shells or ash. Travel on the roads was difficult, especially during heavy rains when it was reported in 1896 that horses sunk up to their knees on the Branford Hills. The Town of Branford spent a lot of money repairing the roads during the year. Each neighborhood had a gang of men that worked on the roads and cleared them after a snow storm.

There was a systematic effort by the town beginning about 1914 to cover or "top dress" the roads. Available materials by that time were McAdam (soil and stone aggregate), tar, Asphalt (bitumen and stone) and concrete (cement and stone). Streets were widened and straightened during the 20th century and sometimes intersections reconfigured. Since the advent of paving, road beds are, in some cases, many inches higher than they were during the 17th and 18th centuries.

It was not until 1907 that the U. S. Supreme Court gave a majority opinion allowing for centralized authority for the development

Streets that are "monumented" indicate the street has been surveyed. Photo by Jane P. Bouley.

The Town of Branford purchased its first truck for road maintenance in 1946.

of roads. The State of Connecticut began a state highway system about 1912 where the towns built, improved, or widened and paid for streets within its boundaries and the state reimbursed some but not all the expense. The state later maintained state designated roads. Examples in Branford are West Main Street, Cedar Street, and Montowese Street. Branford's expense for building or improving these roads for the state was substantial and the work was bonded. The goal of the state highway system was to provide access for military purposes, emergency evacuation, road maintenance, and safe travel between the towns and cities. State roads are termed "monumented" or "non-monumented," that is whether there was ever a concrete or other marker designating its boundary with an official survey. Branford has several state and interstate route numbers- Route 1, I-95, Routes 139, 142, and 146. The designation of New England routes began in 1922 and many were renumbered in 1932. State route numbers became part of the Federal Highway System in 1954 and some route numbers were again changed in 1963.

Some roads maintained by the state were later turned back to the town in 1962. The state at that time took over new portions of roadways. Starting in 1962 Branford was responsible for Main Street and East Main Street between South Main and North Main; Montowese Street from Main to South Main and Leetes Island Road (Route 146) from Route 1 to Thimble Islands Road. The state assumed responsibility for Cedar Street and Brushy Plain Road from North Main to the North Branford line; Elizabeth Street from Limewood Avenue to Pine Orchard Road; Totoket Road from Elizabeth Street to Totoket Road; Totoket Road from Elizabeth Street to Blackstone Avenue; Blackstone Avenue from Pine Orchard Road to Totoket Road and Stony Creek Road from Totoket Road to Thimble Islands Road. The exchange was not without controversy but did pass the Representative Town Meeting.[5]

The National Historic Preservation Act of 1966 established the National Register of Historic Places. In Branford, National Register Districts include Branford Center, Branford Point and Harbor Street, Stony Creek and the Thimble Islands, Canoe Brook, Colonial Houses Thematic District, plus individual listings such as the Branford Electric Railway and Norcross Brothers Granite Quarry. Included on the National Register are scenic highways, Route 146 was designated in 1996.

Laying water pipes on South Montowese Street in 1899. Photo by Harry O. Andrews

Memorial Day parade along Main Street in 1948. Photo by Earl Colter

REPOSITORIES & RESOURCES

The Branford Town Hall, Town Clerk's office, holds the land and town records since the founding of Branford. In addition, the Town Clerk has on file surveyor maps submitted to the town for buildings and developments. The Engineering Department also has zoning, topographical, and other maps. The Assessor Department has maps of streets and buildings.

The James Blackstone Memorial Library has the only complete collection of Branford City Directories, an important resource for 20th century street names. Also available at the library are the local Branford newspapers—*The Branford News, Branford Opinion,* and *Branford Review*. Housed at the library are the archives of the Branford Historical Society which contains some maps and other materials useful in the study of Branford streets and historic buildings.

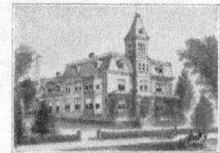

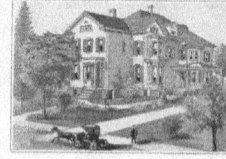

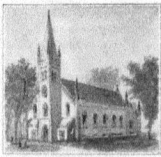

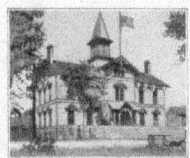

Residence of A. E. Hammer.

Residence and Office of Dr. C. W. Gaylord.

Trinity Episcopal Church.

Branford High School.

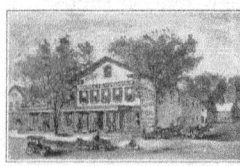

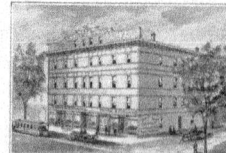

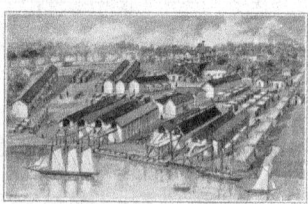

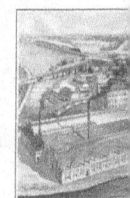

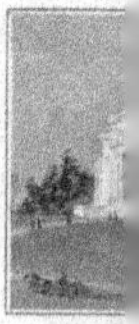

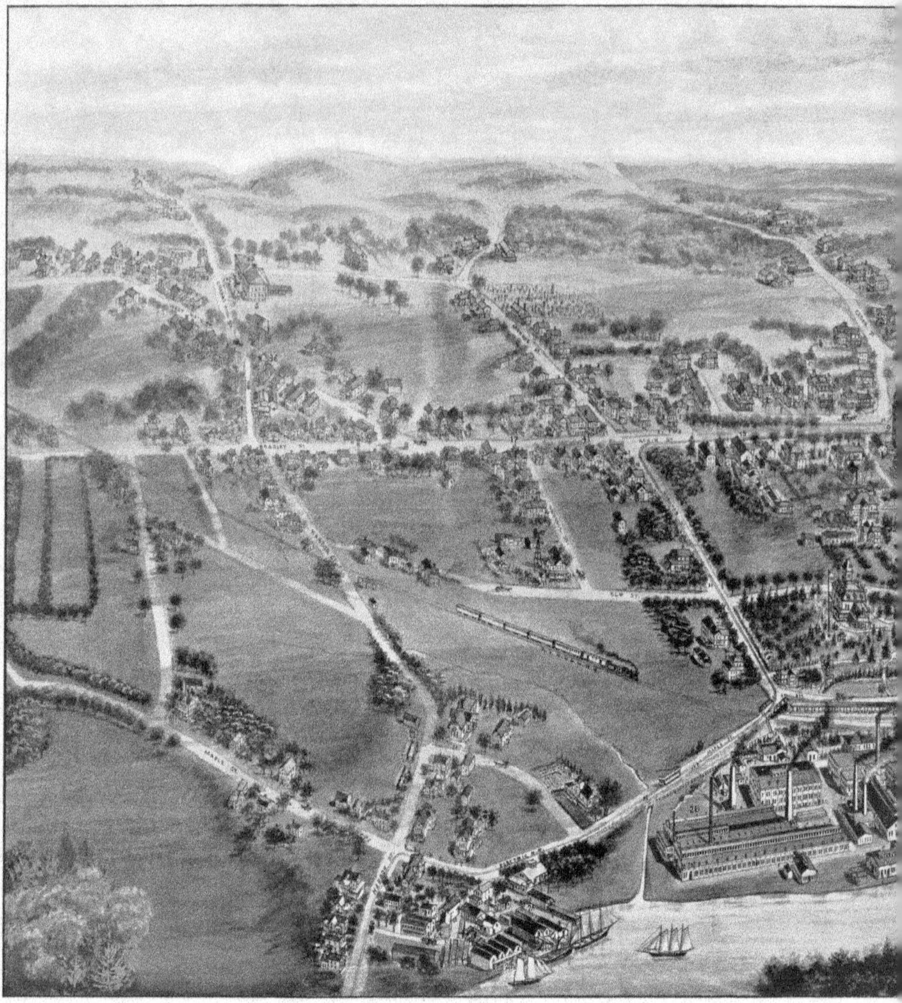

Hoadley & Hutchinson's Block.

Frank & Stannard's Stores, Hosley Block.

F. Jourdan & Son Lumber and Coal Wharf and Yards.

Malleab

M. P. Rice's Stables.

Brang's Bakery. C. F. Mory.

1. Blackstone Memorial Library.
2. Town Hall.
3. Post Office.
4. Branford Station, N. Y., N. H. & H. R. R.
5. Public Schools.
6. First Congregational Church.
7. Trinity Episcopal Church.
8. Baptist Church.
9. Catholic Church.
10. Swedish Evangelical Lutheran Church.
11. Fire Department Buildings.
12. Bradley, Richard. Contractor and Builder, Montowese St.
14. Bohn, Mrs. H. Oak Hall Bottling Works, Main and Chestnut Sts.
15. Brang's Bakery. C. F. Mory, Prop.
16. Clancy, S. S. Stationer and Newsdealer.
17. Clancy, W. S. Undertaker, Main near Monroe St.
18. Doolittle, Edwin. Contractor.
18a. Engquist, A. R. Steam and Hot Water Plumbing, Roofing and Jobbing. Rogers Ave.
19. Gaylord, C. W., M.D. 48 E. Main St.
20. Hanitz, Gustave A. R. Painter and Decorator. Painters' and Artists' Supplies.
21. Higley, W. C. Mason Builder. Jobbing a Specialty. Main St.
22. Hoadley & Hutchinson. Dry Goods, Groceries, Boots and Shoes, Crockery, Hardware, Painters Supplies, Drugs and Medicines.

BR

Hughes &

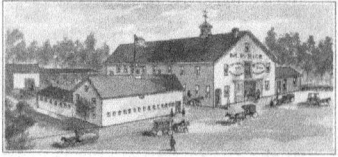

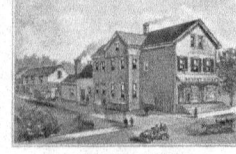

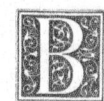

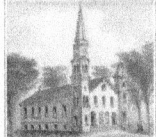

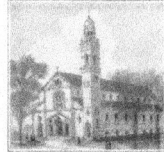

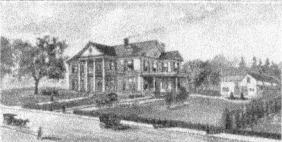

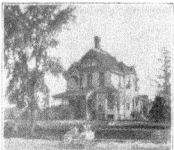

First Congregational Church.

St. Mary's Catholic Church.

Residence and Office of Dr. A. J. Tenney.

Residence of F. Jourdan.

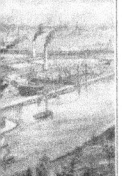

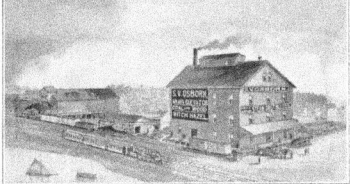

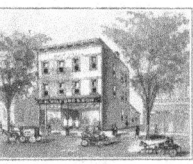

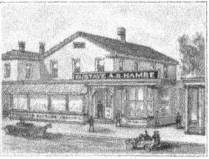

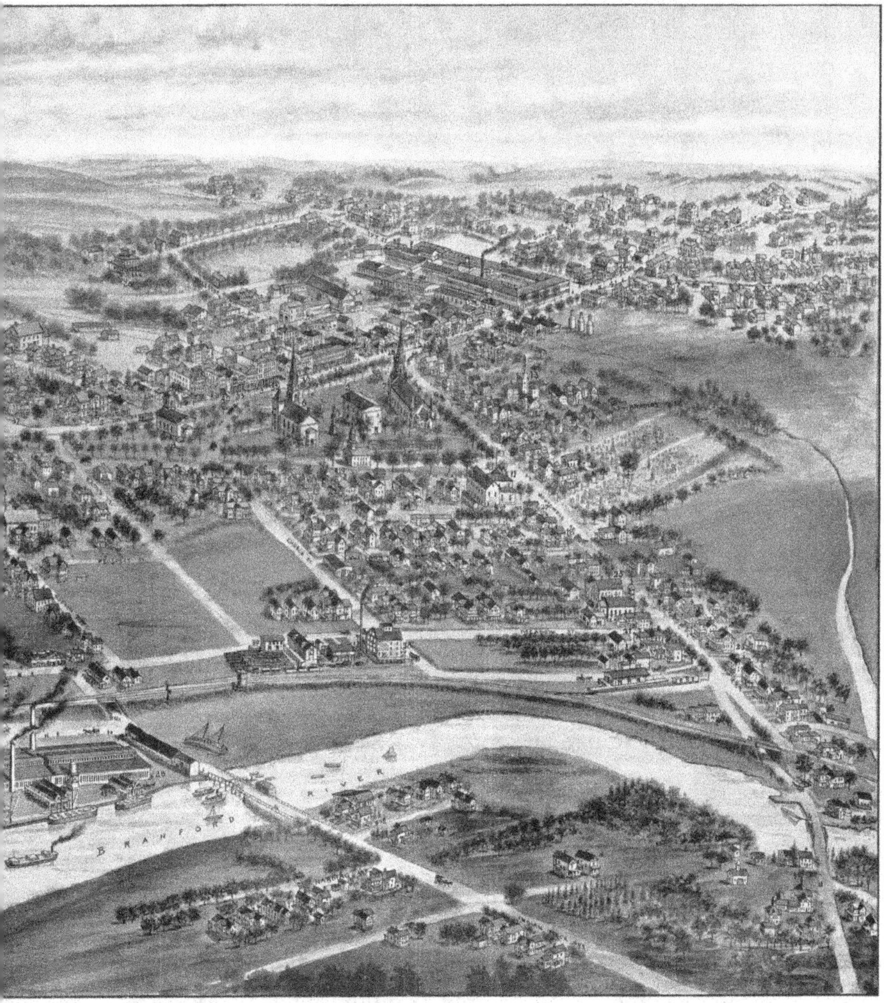

...ctories.

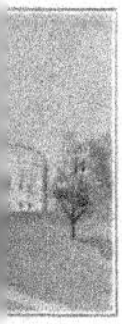

S. V. Osborn, Coal and Lumber, Grain Elevator, Etc.

Chas. H. Wilford's Building.

Gustave A. R. Hamre's Store.

OF

ORD,

T.

... Street, New York.

...Builder, ... Monu...

...d Loan.

..., Flour.

47. Maddern, R. H. Manufacturer and Dealer in Granite and Marble Monuments, Montowese St.

48. Malleable Iron Fittings Co. Mfrs. Air-Furnace Refined Malleable Iron, Steel Castings, Galvanizing, Tinning, Japanning.

49. McCarthy, T. J. Hillside Ave. Cafe, Wines, Liquors and Cigars.

50. Osborn, S. V. Coal, Wood and Domestic Lumber, Grain, Hay, Fertilizers, etc.

51. Prann, F. S. Baker, Rogers Ave.

52. Pronn & Stannard. Groceries, Crockery, Hardware, Paints, Fruits, Confectionery, etc.

53. Porter, Dr. C. H. Dentist, Main St.

54. Rice, M. P. Contractor. Livery and Feed Stables. Grading, Excavating, etc.

55. Rowland, L. Real Estate and Building.

56. Sibley, L. T. Building Stone, Sand, etc. Hack and Livery Stables. Excavating and Carting.

57. Tenney, A. J., M.D. Cor. Main and Laurel Streets.

58. Tobin, T. J. Cafe, Pool and Billiard Rooms; Bottling Works.

59. Totoket Hotel. Jas. O'Connor, Prop.

60. Wilford, Chas. H. General Market; Meats and Provisions.

61. Williams, T. D. Real Estate Agency.

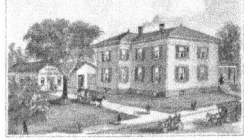

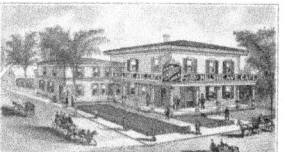

F. S. Prann, Residence and Bakery.

T. J. McCarthy's Hillside Ave. Cafe.

The Connecticut State Library, New Haven Museum, University of Connecticut, Yale University, and other libraries have maps, aerial photographs, and other resources; many of which have been digitized.

CITY DIRECTORIES

Directories for Branford were first published in 1895 by the Price & Lee Company. Price & Lee published the town directories until 1981 but did not produce one every year. In the earlier directories, an alphabetical listing of the town's streets appears in the front of the directory including cross streets. Beginning with the 1928 directory, the streets are listed in the back with every house and their occupants. House numbers are included if they were in use. Also in 1928, a map of the town's streets was included in the directory; most were pulled out and are now missing. Another company began publishing the directories in 1983 and did not include the street index. By examining the city directories chronologically, the development, naming, and renaming of streets during the 20th century can be researched.

DEEDS

Examination of the Branford land records is an essential tool to determine the development of a street or of a specific building.

MAPS

Most streets in this book have a reference map with a number. These refer to the maps in the Town clerk's office at the Branford Town Hall. There is an older set of maps at the Town Clerk's office that are referred to in the book as "old map." Many of these older maps were surveys for the Selectmen concerning new or widening of existing roads before 1920.

Maps Showing Streets and Property Owners

1852   The County of New Haven, A. Budington and R. Whiteford (called the Whiteford map).

PREVIOUS PAGE: The 1905 Bird's-Eye map by Hughes & Bailey shows the streets and buildings in Branford center.

1856   Branford Center, publisher unknown, shows property owners in Branford Center

1856 map, another version, is an updated version of the 1852 map, shows the entire town with property owners. It is part of a much larger hanging map of New Haven County "Map of New Haven County, Connecticut, From actual Surveys, Published by H. & C.T. Smith, No. 17 & 19, Minor St., Philadelphia, 1856

1868   Beers New Haven County Atlas
Two maps, one shows the entire town with property owners and sections for Branford Point, and Stony Creek; the other map is Branford Center.

1881   O. H. Bailey, Bird's-Eye view, shows Branford center with buildings

1905   Hughes & Bailey, Bird's-Eye view, Branford center

Sanborn Maps

D. A. Sanborn founded a map company in 1866 to detail city streets and buildings for the fire insurance industry. The maps are very detailed showing buildings and their footprint. The following is a list of known Branford Sanborn maps. They can be found in various repositories and some have been digitized by Yale University.

   1884, July (2 sheets)
   1889, July (3 sheets)
   1895, September (4 sheets)
   1901, January (8 sheets)
   1908, July (12 sheets)
   1914, January (14 sheets)
   1924, February (24 sheets)

Another version of the 1924 map has 1936 corrections and 1941 corrections.

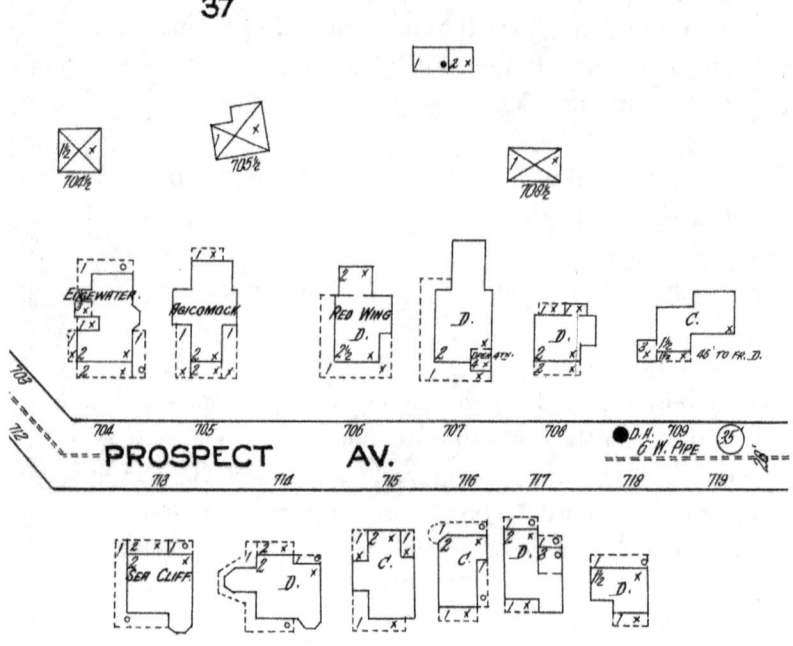

This close-up of the 1914 Sanborn map shows the building configurations and cottage names on Prospect Hill in Stony Creek.

Repositories & Resources

Other Maps of Interest

1892   W. W. Preston and Co. of New Haven

1893   D. H. Hurd & Co. (just Branford center)

1937   Dolph & Stewart 152 West 42nd Street, NYC - New Haven and Environs

   U. S. Coastal and Geodetic Survey (USC&GS) maps and topographical maps

Exchange Club Maps
The Branford Exchange Club produced maps from the 1970s until the 1990s. Some are not dated.

   1976 (red and blue)
   ca 1980 (green)
   ca 1984 (gold)
   ca 1986 (purple)
   1987 (blue)
   1988-1989 (yellow)
   1992 (red)
   1994 (olive)

A variety of other street maps were printed by businesses, the Chamber of Commerce, and other publishers during the last half of the 20th century.

BRANFORD STREETS

ABBOTTS LANE

Branford Center, off Rogers Street to a dead end
Map #165 1973 final plan Abbotts Lane subdivision, Paul B. Abbotts

The street was developed in 1973 and the houses built by Paul B. Abbotts of Branford. The street first appears in the 1976 city directory.

ACETO STREET

Branford Center, off Hamre Lane to a dead end, sometimes Aceto Place
Map #1224 1946 Antonio & Mariatonia Aceto, proposed building lots

Lots were sold by Antonio Aceto over several years and the street was accepted as a town road in 1948[6] from Bertram L. Barker, Jessie M. Albertine, and Antonio Aceto. The street first appears on the 1950 Price & Lee map. Antonio Aceto and his wife Mariatonia D'Onofrio came to Branford about 1909.

Alps Road was a pent road with gates used by the farmers.

The Streets, Alphabetical 17

ACORN ROAD

Off Gould Lane to Beechwood Road
Map #673 1957 Gould Lane, Acorn Industrial site

The street was developed in 1957 by Horace A. L'Heureux and developed further over several decades. It was accepted as a town road in 1959[7] and first appears on the Price & Lee map the same year.

ALEX-WARFIELD ROAD

Branford Hills, off Farm River Road in East Haven to a dead end, sometimes Proprietor's Road
Map #832 1962 Warfield or Proprietor's Road, Map #1059 1973 Warfield property

The street was formerly part of Farm River Road in East Haven and runs parallel to Dominican Road. The Branford portion was a private road and renamed Alex-Warfield Road in 1988 for the John Alex and Charles Warfield families.[8]

ALPS ROAD

Branford Hills and Short Beach, off West Main Street and runs south to Short Beach becoming Clark Avenue

The name first appears in the Town Records in 1692 - "land at a place commonly called by us the alps."[9] It is presumed to be named for the mountains in Europe due to its hilly topography and it was once densely wooded. The road was the only way to get to Short Beach until a bridge was built across the Farm River at East Haven in 1865 and the marsh filled in at Granite Bay. Alps Road was a cart path or pent road with gates or bars that were opened by the farmers to let wagons or livestock through.[10] The road was extended south when Warren Bradley built a house at 381 Clark Avenue in 1849. The road was once steeper and has been graded and straightened several times through the years.

Alps Road was called Old Short Beach Road from the late 1800s until 1930 when the name reverted back to Alps Road. During this period, sometimes just the northern section was called Old Short Beach Road and the southern portion Clark Avenue or the entire stretch still called Alps Road.

Alps Road at the junction of West Main Street was called Plant's Corner when most of Branford Hills was owned and farmed by the Plant family.

ALTMAN STREET

Short Beach, off Court Street to Berger Street
Map #131 1923 a subdivision called Short Beach Manor

Lots were sold over several years by Albert and Caroline (Clark) Altmannsberger of Short Beach. The road first appears on the 1924 Sanborn map. The street was accepted as a town road in 1930[11] when "all roads in Short Beach used by the public" were accepted as town roads. The street name is truncated from Altmannsberger (see also Berger Street). Albert Altmannsberger came to Short Beach in 1893 from Brooklyn, New York and married Caroline Clark. Her father Hiram Clark was a large land owner in Short Beach.

View looking south from Anchorage Road across Elizabeth Street to the water. Shown are the trolley stop and Young family windmill on the right.

The Streets, Alphabetical

ANCHORAGE ROAD

Pine Orchard, off Elizabeth Street north to a dead end,
  sometimes Anchorage Farm Road

The street ran north and south of Elizabeth Street and was a private road owned by the Alden M. Young family. It first appears on the 1924 Sanborn map without a name. The southern section toward the water was a private drive sometimes called Young Road that led to the Young house "The Anchorage." The house was built in 1894 and torn down in 1948.

The northern section off Elizabeth Street led to the family's working farm called Anchorage Farm. The first building was constructed here about 1900. East Road connected to West Road at today's 6 Anchorage Road. The location of the road was changed and constructed east of the original road when the property was developed with new houses and East Road became Anchorage Farm Road. Anchorage Road was accepted as a town road in 1971[12] from the A. M. Young Company.

Alden M. Young, a pioneer in the utility and trolley industry, and his wife Ella Shepardson came to Pine Orchard in the late 19th century eventually purchasing 840 acres. He developed much of the Pine Orchard shoreline and founded the Pine Orchard Yacht and Golf Club. The A. M. Young Company[13] was formed in 1917 after his death to developed and manage the Young family holdings. Many of the streets in Pine Orchard and Damascus were developed by the company which dissolved in 1972.

APPLEWOOD ROAD

Damascus, off Featherbed Lane and circles back out to
  Featherbed, sometimes Applewood Drive
Map #512 1950 lots on Applewood Road

The street was accepted as a town road in 1950[14] from the A. M. Young Company and first appears in the 1953 city directory. The street was developed by the A. M. Young Company as Westwood Acres.

ARK ROAD

Indian Neck, off South Montowese Street to Tabor Drive
Maps #581 & #713 1955 Little Plain subdivision by Bradley,
  Enquist & Williams

Ark Road appears as an unnamed road on the 1852 map with a slightly different configuration leading northeast and connecting to a road south of 18 Pine Orchard Road. This route across the marsh was parallel to South Montowese Street. It was used before the bridge was built across the river from Old Pine Orchard Road.

The Ark lot is referred to in the early 1800s as off Little Plain Road and Ark Road appears by 1888. The 1936 Price & Lee map refers to it as Peter Bridge Road and deeds use both names. The modern Ark Road first appears in the 1939 city directory when the street was extended and lots sold by John S. and Elsa Hendrickson.[15] The street was further developed by Bradley, Enquist & Williams and the extension was accepted in 1957.[16] A small portion on the southerly side was accepted in 1958[17] from August and Mathilde Ritzinger. Another portion of Ark Road was developed in 1966 as the Woodside subdivision.

Clearing Averill Place after a snow storm.

ARROWHEAD LANE

Pine Orchard, off Knollwood Drive to Soffer Place
Maps #924 & #925 1964 Arrowhead development section one

The street was developed in several phases by Joseph and Jacob Soffer, the first portion was accepted as a town road in 1967[18] and an extension in 1970. The street first appears in the 1968 city directory. Another section was developed in 1973 as part of the Indian Woods subdivision by developer Joseph Meshako. Louis Soffer came to Branford about 1920 and purchased the former Town or Poor Farm property in Damascus in 1923.

ASH ROAD

Brushy Plain, off Hemlock Road to Millwood Drive,
   sometimes Ash Creek
Map #783 1960 Ash Road, Brushy Plain

The street was accepted as a town road in 1961[19] from Edward Waltman Associates, Inc. as part of the Millwood development and first appears in the 1962 city directory.

ATWATER EXTENSION

Stony Creek
See Howd Avenue

ATWATER PLACE

Damascus
See Corbin Circle

AVERILL AVENUE OR ROAD

Indian Neck
See Manor Place and Sunset Manor Road

AVERILL PLACE

Branford Center, off Montowese Street to a dead end,
   sometimes Averill Avenue
Map #86 1907 property of Henry Averill, new lots

The street was developed in 1905 by Frederick L. Averill on land belonging to Henry W. Averill of 119 Montowese Street. The development specified the size of the lot, cost of the home, trees planted, width of the street, and restrictions for alcohol sales and commercial enterprises. It first appears in the 1909 city directory. The street is in the National Register Branford Center Historic District. Daniel Averill, a Revolutionary War veteran, came to Branford about 1799 and purchased 87 Montowese Street, now the site of the Armory.

AVON ROAD

Cherry Hill, off Cherry Hill Road to Circle Drive,
    sometimes Avon Avenue
Map #669 1957 development by the Sachs brothers as part of Cherry Hill
    Estates

The street was accepted as a town road in 1958 and an extension in 1960.[20] The street first appears on the 1959 Price & Lee map. Joseph and Esther Sachs came to Branford about 1945 purchasing the former Sagal-Lou Farm. The Sachs family developed much of Cherry Hill over several decades.

BALDWIN PLACE

Pawson Park
See Cottage Street

BALLOU ROAD

Branford Hills, off Alps Road to Eli Yale Terrace
Maps #394 1946 & #385 1948 *Ballou Heights, property of Raymond C.*
    & Edith Y. Ballou, showing Ballou Road, Yale Terrace and Marian Road

The street was accepted as a town road in 1949[21] and first appears in the 1950 city directory. The street was developed and lots sold by Raymond C. and Edith Yale (Prout) Ballou of 32 Alps Road as part of Ballou Heights. The Ballou family came to Branford in 1922.

BARE PLAIN

Bare Plain is a section of North Branford north of Brushy Plain. It was first mentioned in the Branford Town Records in 1695.[22] It is so named because the Indians burned the brush to hunt deer and other animals.

The Streets, Alphabetical 23

BARKER PLACE

Indian Neck, off South Montowese Street to Field Road
Map #473 1950 portion of land of G. Irving Field, proposed streets

The street was accepted as a town road in 1951[23] and first appears in the 1953 city directory. The street was subdivided and named for the Barker family- Ann Barker married George Irving Field (see also Field Place and Field Road).

BARTHOLOMEW ROAD

Indian Neck, off Bishop Road to a dead end

The road first appears on the 1921 map of Waverly Park but is not named. It does not appear as a named street until the 1954 Branford Planning & Zoning map. It is named for brothers Howard and Burton Bartholomew who were builders and original lot owners at Waverly Park.

BARTON COURT

Branford Center, off Palmer Woods Circle to a dead end
Map #1068 1969 the Barwood development

The street was accepted as a town road in 1970[24] and first appears in the 1971 city directory. The developer was Emil Santello and the street was named for his son.

BASSETT ROAD

Short Beach, off Alps Road to a dead end
Map #430 1948 building lots off Alps Road, owner Delbert B. Bassett

The street was accepted as a town road in 1949[25] from Delbert B. Bassett and first appears in the 1953 city directory. The street is named for and was subdivided by Delbert Bassett on land originally belonging to the Warren Bradley family of 381 Clark Avenue.[26]

BATROW LANE

Granite Bay, off Stone Street
Map #1285 1976 refers to Stone Street aka Batrow Lane

A small area of Stone Street is named for the Batrow family of 26 Stone Street. Batrow Lane appears in the city directories and maps in the 1980s. It is really a parking space. John and Vivian Batrow came to Short Beach in 1917.

BAYBERRY LANE

Indian Neck, off Linden Avenue and becomes Summer Island Road, sometimes called Summer Island Road
Map #101 1924 land of the Indian Neck Land Company including Bayberry and Dorr

Cottages were built here by the early 1900s and the street appears on the 1924 Sanborn map. The street was a private road owned by the First Ecclesiastical Society and was accepted as a town road in 1968.[27] The bayberry or wax myrtle is an indigenous plant tolerant of salt water and sandy conditions. The berries were used by the colonists to make candles.

BAYBERRY ROAD

See Berry Patch Road

BAYVIEW AVENUE

Indian Neck, off Fenway Road to Sunset Beach Road
Map #111 1924 Sunset Manor development
Map #708 1950 First Ecclesiastical Society

The street was part of the Sunset Manor development but does not appear until the 1953 Price & Lee map. The street was a private road owned by the First Ecclesiastical Society and was accepted as a town road in 1968.[28]

BEACH AVENUE

Short Beach
See Beckett Avenue

BEACH ROAD

Double Beach
See Sunrise Cove Road

BEACH PLACE

Branford Center, off East Main Street to a dead end

The street first appears in the 1928 city directory and is named for the Samuel Beach family of 94 East Main Street. Elnathan Beach of Stratford came to Branford in 1755 and his cousin Andrew Beach in 1737. The extended families owned property along East Main Street and at Mill Plain. Samuel Beach developed and managed the Pawson Park amusement park.

BEACH STREET

Branford Center
See Hamre Lane

BEACH STREET

Short Beach
See Little Bay Lane

BEAR PATH ROAD

Brushy Plain, off Red Rock Road to Pine Hollow Road
Map #1239 1975 Laurel Hill, owner & developer Herbert Small

The road first appears in the 1976 city directory and was owned and developed by Herbert Small. It was accepted as a town road in 1978.[29]

BEAVER ROAD

Branford Hills, off West Main Street to a dead end
Maps #213 & #239 1929 Beaver Heights, 22 lots, property of Ray U. Plant

The street was accepted as a town road in 1949[30] from Ray U. Plant and first appears in the 1953 city directory. It was named for Beaver Brook or Beaver Swamp that flows into the southeast corner of Lake Saltonstall. Beaver Swamp first appears in the Town Records in 1681.[31]

BECKETT AVENUE

Short Beach, off Clark Avenue east to Bungalow Lane

The street was developed in the 1880s for summer cottages on land owned by Harrison Bristol. It was named for Lucy Beckett of Meriden, one of the early cottage owners. An attempt to make it a town road did not pass in 1897 and the street was later accepted in 1930[32] when "all roads in Short Beach used by the public" were accepted as town roads.

Beckett Avenue originally went from Clark Avenue to Pentecost Street and the eastern portion from Pentecost Street to Bungalow Lane was called Beach Avenue, named for Ebenezer and Eva Beach. Locals called the Beach Avenue portion "Quality Lane" since the houses on the eastern end were more upscale than the western end of the street. Coming down Beckett Avenue from Clark Avenue is "Cook's Hill" sometimes called Cook Avenue, named for Cook family of Plainville and Short Beach. This hill has always been used for sledding. The beach along Beckett Avenue is known as Middle or Long Beach.

The eastern end of Beckett Avenue in 1921. Photo by VanDyke Studio.

BEECHWOOD ROAD

Stony Creek, off Pepperwood Lane to a dead end
Maps #1220 1973 & #1369 1976 part of the Oakledge development

Oakledge was developed by Anderson-Wilcox, Inc. and the street first appears in the 1977 city directory. The owners of the company were John B. Wilcox and Harvey C. Anderson.

BELLAIRE PLACE

Branford Point

The street only appears on the 1924 Sanborn map about half-way down McKinnel Court going north to the Branford River. It correlates with a present day private driveway between 6 & 14 McKinnel Court.

BELLVIEW ROAD

Branford Hills, off Mona Avenue to a dead end
Map #109 1924 Branford Heights, property of Thomas F. Reilly
Map #373 1940 lots on Mona and First Avenue

The street was part of the Branford Heights development and first appears on the 1936 Price & Lee map. It was originally named 1st or First Street (see also Carle Road, Damien Avenue, and Mona Avenue) and was accepted as a town road in 1940[33] from Daniel W. Owens, a real estate agent. The street name was changed in 1958[34] because there was already a First Avenue in Hotchkiss Grove.

BENNETT ROAD

Johnsons Point, an extension of Johnsons Point Road
Map #340 1944 property of Winchester and Susan Bennett

The road was a private drive built in 1904 by M. P. Rice for the Winchester-Bennett family whose house was completed in 1905. It first appears as a street name on the 1944 map but is not listed as an official town road. Bennett Road is now an extension of Johnsons Point Road.

BERGER STREET

Short Beach, off Clark Avenue to a dead end
Map #131 1923 a subdivision called Short Beach Manor

Lots were sold over several years by Albert and Caroline (Clark) Altmannsberger of Short Beach. The road first appears on the 1924 Sanborn map. The street was accepted as a town road in 1930[35] when "all roads in Short Beach used by the public" were accepted as town roads. The street name is truncated from Altmannsberger (see also Altman Street).

BERRY PATCH ROAD

Off Short Beach Road to Linsley Street
*Maps #439 & #468 1948 land developed by Ray U. Plant
   as part of Maple Corners*

The street was accepted as a town road in 1949[36] from Ray U. Plant and first appears in the 1950 city directory. It was originally named Bayberry Road. The street name was changed in 1958 to Berry Patch Lane which was revoked a month later and changed to Berry Patch Road[37] because there was already a Bayberry Lane in Indian Neck.

BIRCH ROAD

Pine Orchard, off Pine Orchard Road to Sunset Hill Road,
   sometimes Birch Drive
Map #1135 1968 the Birchwood subdivision

The street first appears in the 1950 city directory but at that time was only a small section coming off Pine Orchard Road on land belonging to the A. M. Young Company. The entrance off Pine Orchard Road was slightly altered in 1954 and a piece of land exchanged with Frank V. Bigelow.[38] The street was accepted in 1954 as a town road from Bigelow and the A. M. Young Company. The remainder of the road was developed by Christopher Reynolds and Joseph Meshako (R & M Builders) as "Birchwood" and appears on the 1965 Price & Lee map. The street is named for Birch Warner Hincks, grandchild of A. M. Young.

The Streets, Alphabetical 29

BISHOP ROAD

Indian Neck, off Waverly Park Road to a dead end
Map #92 1921 Waverly Park, Fredrick L. Averill

The street was part of the Waverly Park development by Frederick L. Averill of the Indian Neck Land Company. The road appears on the 1921 Waverly Park map and 1924 Sanborn map but does not appear in the city directories or on other maps until 1954. It is named for Elias Gould Bishop.[39]

BLACKSTONE ACRES

See Dogwood Court, Hawthorne Terrace, Jacqueline Way, Oakdale Place, Oakdale Road, Pine Orchard Road, Riverside Drive, Rocky Ledge Lane, Wildwood Drive, and Woodvale Road

Sturgess, Buza & Jockmus Company, Inc. purchased 110 acres in 1954 from descendants of the Blackstone family.[40] The subdivision consisted of 160 homes selling for $14,000 to $17,000 and was the largest development in Branford at that time. The architects were Shilling & Goldbecker of New Haven. The development is named for the Blackstone family; Betsey Jane Blackstone (1835-1926) lived at 18 Pine Orchard Road. John Blackstone came to Branford in 1713 from Rhode Island.

BLACKSTONE AVENUE

Branford Green, off Main Street to South Main Street between the Congregational Church and Baptist Church

A new road was put through the Green by the Village Improvement Society in 1896 named Blackstone Place[41] and appears on the 1924 Sanborn map as Blackstone Avenue. The town reimbursed the Improvement Society for their expenses totaling $200.

BLACKSTONE AVENUE

Pine Orchard, off Totoket Road to Pine Orchard Road
and south to the water
*Map #135 1925 Blackstone Park from the 1910 map with additional
lots on Selden and Yowago*

Blackstone Avenue was part of a proposed 1910 development by A. M. Young known as Blackstone Park including Blackstone Avenue. The town agreed to build the portion of the road north of Pine Orchard Road in 1897[42] but never did. Young instead built it himself in 1898. This portion north of Pine Orchard Road to the former Pine Orchard depot appears on an 1899 map[43] and was called the "road to the Depot." Blackstone Avenue from Totoket Road to Pine Orchard Road became part of the Connecticut State Highway system- Route 146 in 1962[44] and as part of the National Register Route 146 scenic highway in 1996. The street was named for the Blackstone family who had large land holdings in Pine Orchard, most of it eventually purchased by A. M. Young.

Aerial view showing the streets through and around the Branford Green in 1954. Photo by Earl Colter.

The Streets, Alphabetical 31

BLACKSTONE AVENUE

Pine Orchard
See Spring Rock Road

BLACKSTONE PARK

Pine Orchard
Map #23 1907 map of Blackstone Park owned by F. C. Bradley

The Park was a planned development by A. M. Young and F. C. Bradley between Crescent Bluff and Hotchkiss Grove. The land originally belonged to the Blackstone family. Bradley developed and sold lots on Grove, Seldon, Pasadena and Ozone. The Young family developed Yowago Avenue beginning in 1909.

BLACKSTONE'S ROAD

See Pine Orchard Road

BLACKSTONEVILLE

See Hotchkiss Grove Road

BLOCK ISLAND ROAD

Indian Neck, off South Montowese Street ending at the Branford River

The road was developed by the town in 1956[45] when Bruce & Johnson's Marina was built at this location and is named for Casper Block of Branford, an avid recreational fisherman. The street first appears in the 1962 city directory.

BLUESTONE DRIVE

Short Beach, off Shore Drive to a dead end
Map #282 1941 State of Connecticut highway (Shore Drive)

A driveway leading to Altmannsberger Pond to the east of 422 Shore Drive is labeled Bluestone Drive on this map. No other record was found of the name.

The lower Boston Post Road was a colonial road connecting Boston with New York City going through Branford. Photo by Oswin H. Robinson.

The Boston Post Road, also called the Guilford Turnpike, looking west. The house still stands at 675 East Main Street.

BOSTON POST ROAD OR POST ROAD

Branford was on the lower Boston Post Road which was the main colonial route or stage road along the shore from Boston to New York City. The road was called the King's Highway or Great Road.[46] The Post Road was from the Guilford line, along East Main Street, through Branford Center, and over the Branford Hills to East Haven.

The term Boston Post Road was later used in Branford referring to that part of East Main Street east of North Branford Road. This portion was also called the Guilford Turnpike. The Boston Post Road designation was still used on some maps until the 1960s though it was officially East Main Street. Properties along Route 1 in Guilford have a Boston Post Road address.

BOWHAY HILL ROAD

Stony Creek, off Thimble Islands Road to a dead end

The road was originally named Railroad Avenue and was put through about 1885. The street was accepted as a town road in 1925[47] from Elizabeth V. Bowhay. The name Bowhay Hill Road first appears on a 1949 map.[48] The street name was changed in 1958[49] and renamed for the Bowhay family of Stony Creek who came from Cornwall, England in 1871. The street is in the National Register Stony Creek Historic District.

BRADLEY AVENUE

Branford Center, off Montowese Street to a dead end

The street was developed about 1885 and the houses built by brothers F. Cline and Richard Bradley. The land originally belonged to the Blackstone family. The street was accepted as a town road in 1917[50] from Richard Bradley. The street is in the National Register Branford Center Historic District.

BRADLEY AVENUE

Short Beach
See *Court Street*

BRADLEY STREET

Branford Center, off Main Street to a dead end

The road was built in 1691 and named for the Timothy Bradley family whose house still stands at 12 Bradley Street. This section of town was called the Quarter District and was always a mix of residential and commercial use. Besides Bradley, early residents were the Morris, Rose, Parmelee and Bushnell families. The street originally went to Harbor Street then southwest to Short Beach Road but was bisected when the railroad came through in 1852. Bradley Street ended at Maple Street when the latter street was constructed. The southern portion of Bradley Street became Swift Street in 1958. The street is in the National Register Canoe Brook Historic District.

BRAINERD AVENUE

Stony Creek
See Squaw Brook Road

BRAINERD ROAD

Branford Hills, off West Main Street, sometimes Brainard Road
Map #85 1926 Montvale, Lakeview Realty Co., owners Ideal Homes Co.
Map #363 1946 Montvale development

The street first appears in the 1936 directory and was part of the Montvale development. The street was accepted as a town road in 1938[51] from the Lakeview Realty Company and an extension accepted in 1971.[52] A connection for the last name Brainerd could not be made to the early owners or developers.

BRAINERD STREET

Stony Creek
See Thimble Islands Road

BRANDEGEE AVENUE

Pine Orchard, off Island View Avenue
Map #816 1945 Pine Orchard zoning map

The street appears on the 1914 Sanborn map as a driveway and first appears in the 1939 city directory. It is named for William S. Brandegee who owned a "private way" near the Sheldon House in 1890.[53]

BRANFORD

The town was settled in 1644 by families from Wethersfield and New Haven and was originally called Totoket or Totokett for the band of the Quinnipiac who lived here. The name Branford first appears in 1667.[54]

The Branford Green in 1836 showing left to right the first Episcopal church, the Academy now the site of the Town Hall, the Congregational church built in 1744 replaced by the current edifice in 1843. etching by John Warner Barber, Connecticut Historical Collections, New Haven, 1836

Route 1 looking west from Short Beach Road through the section called Plantsville.

The Branford Point Hotel operated from the 1820s until 1914. To the right is lower Harbor Street.

The Streets, Alphabetical 37

BRANFORD GARDENS

Indian Neck
*Map #73 1918 Branford Gardens, owned and developed
  by John J. Linsky, 68 lots*

See Fairlawn Avenue, Garden Street, George Street, Melrose Avenue, and Woodlawn Avenue

BRANFORD GREEN DRIVE

Branford Center
See *Town Hall Drive*

BRANFORD HEIGHTS

Branford Hills

Was a development on property in Branford Hills owned by Thomas F. Reilly and sold by real estate agent Daniel W. Owens. It included Bellview Road, Carle Road, Damien Road, and Mona Avenue.

BRANFORD HILLS

Also called Great Hill, Halfway Hill, Pipestave Hill or Plant's Hill

Branford Hills is the western most section of Branford along the Old Post Road going to East Haven. The eastern portion between Short Beach Road and Alps Road was once called Plantsville.

BRANFORD POINT

See *Harbor Street*

Branford Point is a section of Branford originally called Mulliner's Neck and first appears in the records in 1647.[55] Thomas Mulliner was already living in Branford before the settlers from New Haven and Wethersfield came in 1644. Branford Point is a district on the National Register of Historic Places.

BRANFORD POINT ROAD

See *Harbor Street and Maple Street*

The Malleable Iron Fittings Company (1854-1970) developed several streets in Branford. Photo by Earl Colter.

View of the bridge across the Branford River at East Main Street and Mill Plain Road. Photo by Valdemar T. Hammer.

BREEZY LANE

Off Maple Street to Swift Street

The street was built by the town in 1918[56] but much of the expense was donated by the Malleable Iron Fittings Company (MIF) who owned most of the property. The street first appears in the 1925 city directory and was accepted as a town road in 1935[57] from the MIF. The Malleable Iron Fittings Company was founded at Pages Point in 1854. Thorvald Hammer and others purchased the company in 1864 and members of the family owned and managed the factory until 1968. MIF was the largest employer and taxpayer in Branford producing a wide range of iron and other metal products. The factory closed in 1970.

BRIARWOOD LANE

Branford Hills, off Alps Road and loops back to Alps Road
Map #792 1961 Briarwood, off Alps Road

The street first appears on the 1965 Price & Lee map and was developed in phases by several companies as apartments, condominiums, and homes. The street was accepted as a town road in 1971.[58]

BRIDGE STREET

Branford Center, connects Bradley Street to West End Avenue over the railroad tracks

The street first appears on the 1939 Price & Lee map and before that date was part of West End Avenue. Before Bridge Street was constructed access across the railroad tracks was via an extension of Bradley Street.

BRIDGES

Birch Road - The bridge was replaced in 1989 after being closed to traffic for many years.

East Main Street - One small bridge on East Main Street crosses Queach Brook. The second, also known as Towner's Bridge, at East Main Street and Mill Plain Road, was built in 1687 across the Branford River. Both bridges were replaced in 1916, 1958, and 1989.[59]

Farm River, East Haven River, Stony River or Nellie's Bridge - A bridge across the Farm River connecting East Haven and Short Beach was built about 1865 and was replaced in 1877. A drawbridge was built in 1905 and replaced by the state in 1942. The current bridge was constructed in 1986.

Indian Neck Avenue, Long Bridge, or Upper Bridge - The wooden bridge with pilings was built by 1884. It was rebuilt in 1941 and 1990.

Kirkham Street - This bridge over the railroad tracks was built in 1894 by John Beattie of Leetes Island, Guilford.

Mill Creek - The bridge across Mill or Oyster Creek at Branford Point was first built in 1820 and in 1879 was called the Branford Point Bridge. It was rebuilt in 1880 and in 1934 by the Works Project Administration.

Mill Plain - An old wooden bridge used to connect Flax Mill Road and Mill Plain near the Supply Ponds but washed away and was never replaced.[60]

North Branford Road - A bridge across the river probably dates to the 1700s. A new bridge was constructed in 2017.

Pine Orchard Road or Blackstone Bridge - A wooden bridge was built by the late 1800s over the Branford River at a place called Cart Point. It connected Branford Center to Damascus from Old Pine Orchard Road. The 1918 wooden bridge was removed, and the new bridge relocated in 1962 east of the Armory.

Pine Orchard Road at Knollwood Drive - A bridge was at this location by 1852 when the railroad was built through Branford and appears on the 1852 Whitford map. The bridge was replaced in 1989.

Pleasant Point Road - A bridge above the trolley tracks was built in 1907 and was rebuilt in 1989.

School Ground Road - A bridge over the Branford River was at this location on the 1868 Beers map. The bridge was rebuilt in 1941 by the Works Project Administration and replaced in 2012.

South Montowese Street, Hobart's Bridge or Lower Bridge - This bridge was first built across the Branford River by Samuel Russell in 1791 by private subscription connecting Montowese Street to Indian Neck. It was deeded to the town by the Russell family in 1810. It was rebuilt in 1936 replacing the 1896 old wooden bridge. This bridge has tidal gates.

Sybil Avenue - A bridge across Sybil Creek was built as early as 1812 when the first house on Linden Avenue was built. It appears the current bridge was built just after the 1938 hurricane though the railings have been changed. This bridge has tidal gates.

Waverly Park Road - This bridge over the creek and meadows was built about 1930 when the road was extended.

BRIGHTWOOD LANE

Indian Neck, off Ark Road to a dead end
*Map #967 1967 development by Ernest N. DePoto as the
   Woodside subdivision*

The street first appears in the 1970 city directory.

BRISTOL LANE OR STREET

Short Beach
See Farm River Road and Bristol Street Extension

BRISTOL STREET

Short Beach, off Shore Drive to Beckett Avenue
Map #210 1933 showing original layout of Bristol Street

The street was developed and opened by Harrison Bristol by 1880. The street was accepted as a town road in 1933.[61] It was known locally as Post Office Street when the Short Beach Post Office was at 93 Shore Drive from 1886 to 1924. Harrison Bristol of Cheshire came to Short Beach in 1860 purchasing and developing land in the summer colony.

BRISTOL STREET EXTENSION

Short Beach, north of Shore Drive to a dead end

The street appears on the 1924 Sanborn map but is not named and first appears as a named street in the 1967 city directory. A 1945 map refers to it as Bristol Lane, a private road with one house which still stands today.

BROCKETTS POINT ROAD

Off Short Beach Road to a dead end, sometimes Brockett Road, Dogwood Drive or Wood Road
Map #399 1947 Lanphier Cove Woods, property of Grace Lanphier

Brocketts Point was a summer cottage community developed in the early 1900s by William Elfred Brockett of North Haven. The 1947 map shows Brocketts Point Road as Dogwood Drive. The houses off Short Beach Road were built in 1971 as the "Laurel Woods" development.[62]

BROOKHILLS DEVELOPMENT

Mill Plain

See Brookhills Road, Carriage Hill Road, Coachman Drive, Debra Lane, and Dorchester Lane

BROOKHILLS ROAD

Mill Plain, off Mill Plain Road to Queach Road
Map #672 1955 Brookhills Road, Brookhills, Inc.; layout of a portion of development

The street first appears in the 1942 city directory and was accepted as a town road in 1957[63] from Brookhills, Inc.

BROOKLAWN TERRACE

Branford Hills, off Rose Hill Road to a dead end
Map #717 1941, received 1958 Brooklawn Realty Co., Pleasant View Homes

The street was accepted as a town road in 1949[64] from the Brooklawn Realty Company and first appears in the 1960 city directory.

BROOKWOOD DRIVE

Brushy Plain, off Victor Hill Drive to Side Hill Drive
Maps #927 & #931 1965 Mountain Top Estates owned and developed
   by J. M. DeFelice Construction Company.

The street first appears in the 1967 city directory.

BRUSHY PLAIN ROAD

Connects Cedar Street in Branford to Totoket Road in North Branford

The section of town called Brushy Plain first appears in the Town Records in 1682.[65] It was the main route to the Second Society or North Farms, later called North Branford. The road to North Branford through Brushy Plain was improved in 1712. The end of Brushy Plain Road to the North Branford border has been called Snake Hill for many generations but was previously known as Liddies Hill. Until the mid-twentieth century, most of Brushy Plain was farm land. Brushy Plain Road became a state highway in 1962.[66]

BRYAN ROAD

Branford Point, off Maple Street to Driscoll Road
Old Map #9 1900 building lots A. P., Wm. & S. M. Bryan

The street first appears in the 1913 city directory. The road was built and subdivided by the Malleable Iron Fittings Company on land from Alden P., Scott M. and William Bryan and MIF made the lots available to their employees. The street was accepted as a town road in 1932[67] from the MIF. The street was named for William Bryan of 85 Maple Street whose family owned and operated the Montowese House in Indian Neck. The four-way junction of Maple and Harbor Streets was known as Bryan's Corner and later Jourdan's Corner. The street is in the National Register Branford Point Historic District.

BUCKLEY ROAD

Off Ark Road to a dead end
Map #907 1966 off Ark Road to Branford Building Supplies from
   Catherine Buckley and Mary Jenkin "Little Plain Development"

The street first appears on the 1959 Price & Lee map and is named for John & Catherine (Burke) Buckley.

BUENA VISTA ROAD

Stony Creek, off Thimble Islands Road to a dead end
Old Map #21 1902 proposed layout of road from Flying Point Road to old pent road

The street first appears in the 1913 city directory but was here earlier. A 1909 development off Buena Vista Road called Ozone Park never materialized.[68] Thimble Islands Road between Buena Vista and Wallace Roads was raised in 1962.[69] The street is in the National Register Stony Creek Historic District.

BUNGALOW LANE

Short Beach, off Beckett Avenue to Shore Drive, sometimes Cedar Street, local names were Clam Alley or Lobster Row
Map #275c 1979 Wilcox Estates, Thomas and Mary Doyle

The street name first appears in the 1930 city directory but was here earlier. The street was built to access the compound known as "Bungalow Court" belonging to the poet Ella Wheeler Wilcox whose first home was built in 1891. The street was accepted as a town road in 1930[70] when "all roads in Short Beach used by the public" were accepted as town roads. Before Short Beach was developed, the eastern corner of Bungalow Lane and Shore Drive was used by Jerusha Linsley of Double Beach for her cow pasture.[71] The internationally known poetess Ella Wheeler Wilcox lived year-round in Short Beach until her death in 1919. Bungalow Court was developed into condominiums in 1979.

BURBAN DRIVE

Branford Hills, off Alps Road to Pent road
Map #466 1949 portion of land of Frances Burban

The street was accepted as a town road in 1949[72] from the Burban family and first appears in the 1953 city directory. The land was originally part of the Plant family orchards. Frederick and Frances Burban, natives of Austria, came to Branford Hills about 1916.

The Streets, Alphabetical 45

BURR STREET

Granite Bay, off Grove Street and becomes Hill Street,
   sometimes Burr Place

The street first appears in the 1930 city directory though houses were built here earlier. It is named for William A. Burr, an early resident of Granite Bay. Near Burr Street and Sherwood Street was a road or path called Smugglers Road, said to be used during Prohibition. Smugglers Road appears on Goggle maps (2016) on the west side of Grove Street between Stone and Union Streets to a dead end.

BUSINESS PARK DRIVE

Off East Main Street to Leetes Island Road

The street was developed in 1971 as part of the Cosgrove Industrial Park subdivision.

BUTTERMILK LANE

Mill Plain, off Ramblewood Road and loops back to Ramblewood
Map #1018 1969 as part of the "Ramblewood" subdivision

The street was accepted as a town road in 1964[73] and first appears in the city directory the same year. It was originally called Shelly Ann Road on the subdivision map.

CADWELL PLACE

Mill Plain, off Windmill Hill to a dead end
*Maps #396 1947, #407 1948 & #414 1949 land of Adelia M. Cadwell,
   widow of Ernest*

The street was a private road and first appears on the 1950 Price & Lee map. Ernest W. and Adelia (Butler) Cadwell came to Branford about 1916 from Hartford.

CAMP HILL

Stony Creek
See Prospect Hill Road

CANOE BROOK

Branford Center

Canoe Brook according to legend was the width of a canoe. The name first appears in the Town Records in 1669.[74] It also refers to a section of Branford where the brook ran, from Cherry Hill Road west along Main Street and north to the current North Main Street. The brook is now covered by roads and development. Before North Main Street was built there was a small bridge to cross the Canoe Brook. The Canoe Brook neighborhood was recognized as a National Register Historic District in 2001.

CAPTAINS LANE

Branford Point, off Stannard Avenue to a dead end
Map #855 1963 Captains Lane, two building lots

The street first appears on the 1950 Price & Lee map and is probably named for several generations of the Stannard family who were boat captains.

CARLE ROAD

Branford Hills, off Mona Avenue to a dead end
Map #109 1924 Branford Heights, property of Thomas F. Reilly

The street first appears on the 1936 Price & Lee map and was originally named 2nd or Second Street (see also Bellview Road, Damien Avenue, and Mona Avenue) and was part of the Branford Heights development. It was accepted as a town road in 1939[75] from Daniel W. Owens, real estate agent. The street name was changed in 1958[76] because there was already a Second Avenue in Hotchkiss Grove.

CARRIAGE HILL DRIVE

Mill Plain, off Queach Road to a dead end, sometimes Carriage Hill
  Road or Carriage Drive
Map #880 1963 development by Anderson-Wilcox, Inc.

The street was accepted as a town road in 1966[77] and first appears in the city directory the same year. It was part of the Brookhills, Inc. development, a subdivision called Carriage Hill.

The Streets, Alphabetical 47

CASTLE ROCK

Branford Point, off Stannard Avenue to a dead end

Castle Rock was a mansion owned by William H. and Frances Inman of Virginia overlooking the Branford Harbor. After the death of Willie Lee Inman the property was sold in 1967 and the Castle Rock condominiums built.[78] The Condominiums have a Castle Rock address.

CEDAR HILL

Stony Creek
See Lavassa Terrace

CEDAR STREET

Branford Center, off Main Street going north becoming Brushy Plain Road

The street appears on the 1852 map as one of the routes from Branford Center to North Branford. A portion of Cedar Street was accepted as a town road in 1932[79] from Lucy A. and Margaret A. Sullivan and was widened at that time. Part of the street was relocated and reconstructed in 1961.[80] The portion from North Main Street north became a state highway in 1962.[81] The street south of North Main Street is in the National Register Branford Center Historic District.

CEDAR STREET

Indian Neck
See Hemingway Street

CENTRAL AVENUE

Stony Creek
Map #63 Governors Island, no date

Central Avenue appears on this map of Governors Island.

CHAPEL DRIVE

Pine Orchard, off Pine Orchard Road to Island View Avenue

The street was originally named Park Place because it was on the "park side" of the proposed Blackstone Park development (see Blackstone Avenue, Pine Orchard). The street name was changed in 1958[82] because there was already a Park Place in Branford Center. It was renamed for the Pine Orchard Union Chapel which faces the street and was built in 1896.

CHERRY HILL

Cherry Hill is a section of Branford between Branford Center and Branford Hills and was originally called Littleworth. A home was built here in 1734 by Samuel Barker and it became known as Cherry Hill about 1845 when James F. Morris planted 300 imported cherry trees. The last of the original cherry trees was destroyed during the 1938 hurricane. Cherry Hill was developed in the mid to late 20th century.

Aerial view of the development of Cherry Hill Estates showing the former Sagal Lou farm in 1956. Photo by Earl Colter.

CHERRY HILL CIRCLE

See Montoya Drive and Circle, sometimes Sagal Lou Road
Maps #544 & 572 1954 layout of Cherry Hill Circle, Cherry Hill Apartments, property of the Sachs Brothers

The street was accepted as a town road in 1956[83] from Cherry Hill Apartments, Inc. and first appears on the 1959 zoning map. The name was changed about 1986 and is now called Montoya Circle and Drive.

CHERRY HILL ESTATES

Map #336 1945 property of Dorothy Rodney, Sagal Realty Corp.
Map #668 1957 Sachs Brothers development

Much of Cherry Hill was developed in several phases by the Sachs family including a shopping center, apartments, and private homes. The land was formally the dairy farm of Louis Sagal that was sold by his daughter Dorothea Rodney (Sagal Realty Corp.) to the Sachs brothers in 1946.

CHERRY HILL ROAD

Off Main Street extending north to a dead end, also Branford Road, sometimes Cherry Hill Street

The street is a colonial road originally called Blatchley Cartway and "towards Blatslys bars" is first mentioned in the Town Records in 1662[84] and Cartway in 1681. Thomas Blatchley was a first settler of Branford and moved to Guilford about 1668. The name Cherry Hill Road was used by 1868. The street originally went through to the Hosley farm on Hosley Avenue. This northern portion was abandoned about 1965 and the street is now a dead end though the abandoned part of the road can still be seen. The street south of North Main Street is in the National Register Canoe Brook Historic District.

CHERRY STREET

Branford Center, off Cherry Hill Road to Monroe Street,
   sometimes Sullivan Road or Street
Map #32 1911 Monroe Street Extension, land of Jeremiah Sullivan

The street was put through by the town in 1882[85] and first appears on the 1893 Hurd map. The street was extended in 1892.[86] It appears on the 1924 Sanborn map as Sullivan Street but is listed in the city directories as Cherry Street. Some of the land belonged to Daniel and Jeremiah Sullivan. The Sullivans were among the early Irish settlers of Branford.

CHESTNUT STREET

Branford Center, off East Main Street to Short Rocks Road

The street was here by 1750 connecting Branford Center to Short Rocks. The Supply Ponds were built by the New Haven Water Company at the end of Chestnut Street in 1899.[87] Sometimes the upper section is called North Chestnut Street. The street south of North Main Street is in the National Register Branford Center Historic District.

CHURCH STREET

Branford Center, off South Main Street to Meadow Street

The First Congregational Church purchased the land in 1885,[88] subdivided and sold the lots beginning in 1886. The church built the Manse[89] in 1889 at 75 South Main Street. The street was widened and regraded in 1907. Some of the street was accepted as a town road in 1932 from the Atlantic Wire Company. The street is in the National Register Branford Center Historic District.

CIDER MILL LANE

Off Stannard Avenue to Harbour Village
Map #724 1958, property of Ray U. Plant called Plant's Rock Pasture

The street first appears in the 1965 city directory. The street was further developed in 1975 and this portion accepted as a town road in 1977.[90] Many families in Branford made and sold cider.

The Streets, Alphabetical 51

CINDER DRIVE

Indian Neck
See Haycock Point

CIRCLE DRIVE

Cherry Hill, off Greenfield Road to Avon Road
Map #669 1957 as part of Cherry Hill Estates

The street first appears on the 1959 Price & Lee map.

CLANCY ROAD

Off North Main to a dead end
Maps #187 1932 & #1074 1942 property of William S. Clancy

It is a private road originally the property of William S. Clancy who gave lots to family members. The first house was built in 1941. The street name first appears in the 1973 city directory. James and Eliza (Regan) Clancy were among Branford's first Irish settlers coming about 1855.

CLAREDON STREET

Branford Hills, off Matthew Road to Brainerd Road
Map #85 1926 Montvale, Lakeview Realty Co., owners Ideal Homes Co.

The street is named on the 1926 development plan for Montvale and first appears on the 1953 Price & Lee map.

CLARK AVENUE

Short Beach
See Pentecost Street

CLARK AVENUE

Short Beach, an extension of Alps Road going south
  across Shore Drive to a dead end

The portion south of Shore Drive was put through in 1852 when Harrison Bristol built a summer hotel overlooking "Short Beach," today called Johnsons Beach. It was originally just called the Shore Road and was eventually named for Hiram Clark, an early Short

Beach property owner. In 1880 "a new road is to be built to Short Beach from where Alps Road ends."[91] This was the portion of Clark Avenue north of Shore Drive. The street was accepted as a town road in 1930[92] when "all roads in Short Beach used by the public" were accepted as town roads. The name Clark Avenue first appears on the 1930 Price & Lee map but was probably used earlier. The end of Clark Avenue is called Paynes Point.

CLUB PARKWAY

Pine Orchard, off Chapel Drive to Waterside Road

The street was built when the Pine Orchard Club house was moved from Totoket Road to its current location in 1916. The street does not appear on the 1914 Sanborn map.

COACHMAN DRIVE

Mill Plain, off Queach Road to Carriage Hill Drive
*Map #880 1963 part of the Carriage Hill development built
  by Anderson-Wilcox, Inc.*

The street was accepted as a town road in 1966[93] and first appears in the city directory the same year. It was part of the Brookhills, Inc. development, a subdivision called Carriage Hill.

COCHECO AVENUE

Indian Neck, off Linden Avenue to a dead end

The street was built before 1903 when the "Cocheco cottage" was already here. The origin of the street name is not known, however, there is an Abenaki Indian word Cocheco believed to mean rapid foaming water. There is a river by the name in New Hampshire.

COLLINS DRIVE

Pine Orchard, off Pine Orchard Road to a dead end
*Map #384 1946 property of Nellie I. Collins, 20 building lots
Map #1025 1968 Oak Hollow, section one, owned and developed by
  Christopher Reynolds and Joseph Meshako (R & M Builders)*

The street was accepted as a town road in 1948[94] from Nellie (Sullivan) Collins of 101 Pine Orchard Road and first appears on

The Streets, Alphabetical 53

the 1950 Price & Lee map. The street was further developed in 1968. She was the daughter of Jeremiah Sullivan of Cherry Street and the widow of Michael Collins.

COMMERCIAL PARKWAY

Cherry Hill, off North Main Street to a dead end, sometimes
   Commerce Park Road
Map #1548 1979 developed by Hamilton Branford Limited Partnership

The southern portion was originally named Cherry Hill Circle. The new name first appears in the 1988 city directory.

COMMERCIAL STREET

Off Route 139 to a dead end
*Map #1024 1972 land to Cosgrove Development Co., Inc.
   from Irving Korman, Jr.*

The street was built as an industrial park and first appears in the 1976 city directory.

CONNECTICUT TURNPIKE

Officially called the Governor John Davis Lodge Turnpike,
   also Interstate 95 or I-95

The toll road through Connecticut was one of the highway construction projects completed throughout the country in the 1950s. The State of Connecticut by imminent domain purchased tracts of land in 1953 from Branford residents to build what was called the Greenwich-Killingly Expressway. The portion through Branford was not without controversy, going through neighborhoods and farm land where several historic buildings, especially at Mill Plain and in the Paved Street District were torn down.

   Construction on the Connecticut Turnpike began in 1954 and was opened on January 2, 1958.

   During the 18th and 19th centuries a turnpike referred to a toll road, often privately owned, where a turnstile or gate with four cross bars was used to collect the payment and the road had an end or "pike." The term turnpike became a catch phrase for these types of toll roads. Between 1795 and 1953 there were 121 turnpike franchises in Connecticut but none in Branford.[95]

The Branford toll station on the Connecticut Turnpike was near Exit 53. Toll booths in Connecticut were removed in 1985.

Bradley Avenue in Short Beach was renamed Court Street in 1958.

The Streets, Alphabetical 55

CORBIN CIRCLE
Damascus, off Damascus Road to a dead end

The street was originally called Atwater Place when it was proposed in 1966. The street was accepted as a town road in 1970 and the name changed at that time.[96] The street first appears in the 1973 city directory and was developed by Fred Corbin.

COTTAGE STREET
Indian Neck, off Pawson Road in both directions to dead ends
Map #201 1933 change of leaseholder of a portion of Pawson Park

The street was originally named Grove Place or Street and first appears on Map #201 but cottages were here earlier. The map shows a right of way connecting Spring Cove Road and Cottage Street called Baldwin Place. The street name was changed in 1958[97] because there already a Grove Avenue in Pine Orchard and a Grove Street in Granite Bay. The street was a private road owned by the First Ecclesiastical Society and was accepted as a town road in 1968.[98]

COURT STREET
Short Beach, off Shore Drive to Clark Avenue

The street was originally named Bradley Avenue for the Warren Bradley family of 381 Clark Avenue, the first year-round home in Short Beach. The street was here by 1893 and the name changed in 1958[99] because there was already a Bradley Avenue in Branford Center. It was renamed for the tennis courts which once stood where the entrance to Altman Street is today. The street was accepted as a town road in 1930[100] when "all roads in Short Beach used by the public" were accepted as town roads.

COVE TERRACE
Branford Point, off Stannard Avenue to a dead end
Map #535 1954 land of William H. Crawford

The street first appears on the 1950 Price & Lee map.

CREEK COURT

Indian Neck, off Waverly Park Road to a dead end

Cottages were built here about 1930 and the street first appears as Waverly Lane in the 1936 city directory. The street does not appear on the 1921 Waverly Park map. The new name first appears in the 1962 city directory.

CRESCENT BLUFF AVENUE

Pine Orchard, off Pine Orchard Road to a dead end
Old Map #1 1885 Plan of 35 building lots belonging to E. B. Baker

Crescent Bluff or just The Bluff was developed by Ellis B. Baker who subdivided and sold lots beginning in 1885.[101] It is named for the crescent shaped beach at the end of the road. Crescent Bluff also referred more generally to the waterfront east and west of the Avenue and included The Anchorage, home of the A. M. Young family. Baker was a telephone pioneer opening a telephone exchange in Meriden in 1872, said to be the second in the world.

Crescent Bluff Ave., Looking North.

Crescent Bluff Avenue was developed by Ellis B. Baker in 1885.

CREST AVENUE

Short Beach
See Riverview Avenue

CRESTWOOD ROAD

Brushy Plain, off Laurel Hill to a dead end

The street was built in 1974 as part of the Laurel Hill subdivision and was accepted as a town road in 1976.[102]

CROSSWOODS DRIVE

Branford Hills
See The Greens

CROUCH ROAD

Indian Neck, off Limewood Avenue to Waverly Park Road
Map #71 1918 land to the Indian Land Co. from Albert H. Crouch

The street was developed by Frederick L. Averill, manager of the Indian Neck Land Company and first appears on the 1924 Sanborn map. Crouch Road is referred to in deeds as a right of way when lots were sold by Frederick Averill at Waverly Park in 1921. Edward and Margaret Crouch came to Branford in 1867 from Brooklyn, New York.

CURVE STREET

Off Maple Street to Harbor Street

Some of the houses on the street were built in the 1880s and the street is not on the 1881 Bird's-Eye map, but is on the 1905 map. The name first appears in the 1913 city directory. It is named for the nearly ninety-degree left hand turn halfway down the street. The street is in the National Register Branford Point Historic District.

CYPRESS DRIVE

Brushy Plain, off Hemlock Road becoming Fresh Meadow Road

The street was accepted as a town road in 1961[103] from Edward Waltman Associates, Inc. and first appears in the 1962 city directory as part of the Millwood development.

DAMASCUS

Damascus is a section of Branford the name of which appears in the Town Records by 1741.[104] It refers to the Damascus Road, Windmill Hill, and Featherbed Lane area and early settlers were the Hoadley and Blackstone families. It may refer to Damascus, the capitol of Syria, or on "the road to Damascus" and relates to the conversion of Paul the Apostle.

DAMASCUS ROAD

From Pine Orchard Road to Totoket Road
See also Pine Orchard Road

Various sections of Damascus Road have had different names during various time periods.

Parting Paths - The intersection of Pine Orchard Road and Damascus Road in front of 6 Damascus Road was for a century or more known as Parting Paths.[105] Sometimes it is called Parting Paths Road. This intersection has been reconfigured several times, the last was in 1988.

Parting Paths, the junction of Damascus and Pine Orchard Roads, was reconfigured in 1988. Photo by Jane P. Bouley.

Poor House Road - When the Town Poor House[106] was on Damascus Road from 1874 until 1921, the section from Parting Paths to Windmill Hill Road was known as Poor House Road. Even as late as 1932 it was still referred to with that name.

Stony Creek Road - The section from Windmill Hill Road going toward Stony Creek and Pine Orchard (in front of today's Welch or Middle School) was called Stony Creek Road.

Damascus Road - It was the name of the road from Parting Paths to Windmill Hill Road (and included what was called Poor House Road). For decades Damascus Road was also called Old Stony Creek Road. In 1958[107] the entire stretch from Pine Orchard Road (at Parting Paths) to the intersection of Stony Creek Road and Totoket Road was designated as Damascus Road.

DAMBERG PLACE

Branford Center, off Montowese Street to a dead end

The street first appears in the 1930 city directory and is named for the Damberg family. The street is in the National Register Branford Center Historic District.

DAMIEN ROAD

Branford Hills, off Mona Avenue to a dead end

The street was accepted as a town road in 1940[108] from Daniel W. Owens and first appears on the 1950 Price & Lee map. It was originally named 3rd or Third Avenue (see also Carle and Bellview Roads). The street name was changed in 1958[109] because there was already a Third Avenue in Hotchkiss Grove. The origin of the name was not determined.

DEBRA LANE

Mill Plain, off Brook Hills Road to a dead end
Map #950 1966 Brookhills, Inc. West

The street first appears in the 1970 city directory (with no houses) and was accepted as a town road in 1971.[110]

DEEPWOOD PARK
Short Beach

There was a small section on the south side of Shore Drive from Clark Avenue toward the Farm River known as Deepwoods or Deepwood Park where 17 & 19 Shore Drive are today.

DEEPWOOD ROAD
Pine Orchard
See Meadow Wood Road

DEFOREST DRIVE
Mill Plain, off Queach Road, loops then divides and becomes Brook Road and Glen Road
Map #606 1956 subdivision Cedar Lake Acres, Cedar Lake Construction Co., owner and developer DeForest & Hotchkiss

The street first appears on the 1956 Price & Lee map and was accepted as a town road in 1958[111] from Cedar Lake Construction Company. The DeForest & Hotchkiss Lumber Company was established in New Haven in 1852 by Andrew W. DeForest and Justus S. Hotchkiss. Purchasing the company was Josiah G. Venter of Johnsons Point and during the 1950s Rudolph F. Bailey of Branford was an officer.

DOGWOOD COURT
Blackstone Acres, off Pine Orchard Road to a dead end
Map #663 1956 Blackstone Acres section two, owner and developer Buza, Sturgess & Jockmus, Inc.

The street was accepted as a town road in 1958[112] and first appears in the city directory the same year.

DOGWOOD DRIVE
Brocketts Point
See Brocketts Point Road and Rustic Road

The town accepted Laurel Road, Dogwood Drive, and Howard Avenue at Lanphiers Cove in 1947.[113]

DOMINICAN ROAD

Branford Hills, off West Main Street to a dead end
Map #538 1954 owner and developer James J. Canna

The street was accepted as a town road in 1956[114] from James J. Canna (C & C Construction) and first appears in the city directory the same year. The land was sold by the Devlin family to Canna.

DORCHESTER LANE

Mill Plain, off Northford Road to a dead end
Map #922 1965, sections two and three of the Brookhills, Inc. development

The street was accepted as a town road in 1972[115] and first appears in the 1973 city directory.

DORR STREET

Indian Neck, from Pawson Road to Bayberry Lane
Map #302 1913 building lots Pawson Park Road corner of Linden Avenue
Map #101 1924 property of the Indian Neck Land Company

Lots were laid out in 1913 and the street appears on the 1924 Sanborn map. It was originally called Second Street and the street name was changed in 1958[116] because there was already a Second Avenue in Hotchkiss Grove. The street is named for the Dorr family who owned one of the cottages. The street was a private road owned by the First Ecclesiastical Society and was accepted as a town road in 1968.[117]

DOUBLE BEACH

Also called Town Neck

Double Beach is a section of Branford and is named for the sandbar leading to Love Island which at low tide exposes two beaches. The only inhabitants in this area of Branford in the early 1700s were the Lanphier and Linsley families. There is a tradition that the first settlers of Branford met here under an oak tree in 1644.

DOUBLE BEACH ROAD
Off Short Beach Road to a dead end

A road to the Lanphier and Linsley farms at Double Beach appears on the 1710 Bradley map. In a 1900 deed it was referred to as "the pent highway to Lanphiers Cove known as Double Beach Road."

DOUBLE BEACH ROAD
Branford Point
See Harbor Street

DRISCOLL ROAD
Branford Point, off Maple Street to Harbor Street
Map #159 1929 land of Mary E. Driscoll to the Malleable Iron Fittings Co.
Map #244 1936 Driscoll Road

The street first appears in the 1930 city directory and was accepted as a town road in 1936 from the Malleable Iron Fittings Co. and part in 1939[118] from G.A.R. Hamre. Daniel and Catherine (Harrington) Driscoll were among the Irish immigrants settling in Branford about 1855.

Double Beach Road was one of the first streets in the western section of Branford, appearing by 1710.

The Streets, Alphabetical 63

DUDLEY AVENUE

Hotchkiss Grove, off First Avenue to Elizabeth Street
Map #152 1914 Hotchkiss Grove and Pine Orchard West

The 1914 map refers to New Dudley Avenue with ten lots and a forty-foot road. The street appears on the 1924 Sanborn map but most of the homes were built much later. The road was named for Mary Louisa Dudley, mother of Emerson M. Hotchkiss.

DUTCH HOUSE QUARTER

Also called Dutch Wharf, Dutch House Point, Dutch House Neck

Reference to the Dutch House first appears in the Town Records in 1671.[119] Today Dutch Wharf Marina is at 70 Maple Street.

EADES STREET

Branford Center, off South Main Street to Prospect Street
Map #4 1903 proposed street (Eades Street)

The street was laid out in 1903 on land belonging to John Eades and Hattie Thompson. Part of the road was already there as a private drive to access the rear of the homes on South Main Street (which may be the same as Tyler Place, see below). The road was widened when the High School (now Sliney School) was built in 1928. John Eades was born in England and came to Branford in 1870.

Tyler Place is referred to in the town annual reports and early city directories as "from South Main near Main" and appears to be a short road or driveway about where Eades Street was put through. The 1913 city directory lists "Tyler Place, see Eades Street."

The little cut through the Green north of Eades Street connecting South Main Street and Main Street was built in 1904 and a former little road on the west side of the Green called "Misplaced Alley" was eliminated.

EAST INDUSTRIAL DRIVE

Off East Main Street to School Ground Road

The street first appears in the 1978 city directory and was part of the Cosgrove Industrial Park.

EAST MAIN STREET

From the intersection of Main, Ivy, and Chestnut Streets east to the Guilford line, also called Boston Post Road, Guilford Turnpike, Old Guilford Turnpike, Guilford Road, King's Highway, Main Road, Post Road, Old Post Road, Route 1

East Main Street is a colonial road that was part of the lower Boston Post Road connecting Boston to New York City. The portion from Branford Center to North Branford Road (Route 139) was called East Main Street and east to the Guilford line was called The Guilford Turnpike or just the turnpike. This eastern section was called Main Road in the 1910 census. Some or all was at different times called the Boston Post Road. The name East Main Street was officially reset in 1958 as running from Chestnut Street to the Branford-Guilford line.[120] Even after 1958 some maps still called the east portion Boston Post Road. East Main Street east of Featherbed Lane became as state road in 1906.[121] The portion from North Main Street to Main Street is in the National Register Branford Center Historic District.

ECHLIN STREET

Branford Hills, off West Main Street to a dead end
Map #757 1961 property of Echlin Manufacturing Co.

Echlin Manufacturing Company purchased nineteen acres in 1955 off Alps Road from the Harrison-Jones family and built a manufacturing complex. The street first appears in the 1962 city directory.

EDGEWOOD DRIVE

Blackstone Acres
See Wildwood Drive

EDGEWOOD STREET

Granite Bay, off Forest Street to Stone Street, sometimes Edgewood Road

The street was put through in 1906 as Forest Street when Granite Bay was developed. The name Edgewood first appears on the 1950 Price & Lee map. It is called both Stone Street and Forest Street during the 1950s and back to Edgewood on a 1965 map. Today the street has only two houses that have both an Edgewood and Forest Street address.

The Streets, Alphabetical 65

EIGHTH AVENUE

See *Hotchkiss Grove*

ELI YALE TERRACE

Branford Hills, off Ballou Road to Marion Road
Maps #394 1946 & #385 1948 Ballou Heights, property of Raymond C. & Edith Y. Ballou

The street was developed and lots sold by Raymond C. and Edith (Prout) Ballou of 32 Alps Road as part of Ballou Heights. It was originally named Yale Terrace or Yale Street and named for Marian (Yale) Prout, mother of Edith Ballou. The street was accepted as a town road in 1949[122] and first appears in the 1950 city directory. The street name was changed in 1958[123] with the addition of Eli because there was already a Yale Court in Short Beach. Yale was a family name and the addition of Eli associating it with Yale University is a misnomer.

East Main Street showing the popular Oasis Restaurant in 1950, now the site of the United Methodist Church.

ELINOR PLACE

Off Alps Road to a dead end
Map #153 1928 property of George C. Kirkham and William R. Foote

The street was developed in 1928 and first appears on the 1939 Price & Lee map. Kirkham was a real estate agent from East Haven and Foote a banker and property owner in Branford. Elinor Kaiser was the wife of Henry Kaiser who built the houses.

ELIZABETH STREET

Pine Orchard, connects Hotchkiss Grove Road to Pine Orchard Road on Route 146 then south to the water to a dead end

On the 1868 map Hotchkiss Grove Road and Pine Orchard Road both went south to the Pine Orchard shoreline to a few waterfront houses. There was no cross street between the two. Elizabeth Street was put through after 1901[124] when Pine Orchard residents requested it be built and appears on the 1907 Blackstone Park development map. It was accepted as a town road in 1920.[125] It is named for Elizabeth (born 1881), the youngest daughter of A. M. Young. The southern portion going to the water appears on the 1924 Sanborn map as a private road. Part of Elizabeth Street to Blackstone Avenue was a state road by 1917.[126] Elizabeth Street became part of the Connecticut State Highway system - Route 146 in 1962[127] and as part of the National Register Route 146 scenic highway in 1996.

ELM STREET

Branford Center, off Rogers Street west to North Harbor Street

The street first appears on the 1868 Beers map but only running from Rogers Street to Kirkham Street. By 1881 the street was extended west to North Harbor Street though very few houses were built yet along this new section. Once covered in a canopy of elm trees, only one old elm tree remains. The centerpiece of the east side of Elm Street was the estate of Alfred E. Hammer called "Elverhoi," in Danish meaning elves hill. It faced Elm Street and was centered between Kirkham and Rogers Streets, the rear overlooking the train station and the Malleable Iron Fittings Company (MIF). Hammer was an inventor, treasurer, and general manager of the MIF. After his death, the home was razed in 1939 and the property purchased

The Streets, Alphabetical   67

by Smithfield Engineering Company and developed with single family homes. Remnants of the stone pillars can still be seen. There were several phases of building along Elm Street. The street is in the National Register Branford Center Historic District.

ELM STREET
Stony Creek
See Three Elms Road

ELY STREET
Branford Point, off Harbor Street to a dead end, sometimes Ely Lane
Map #582 1943 property of Esther Ely

Hervey Frisbie's shipyard, also called Brown's Wharf, is marked on the 1852 Whiteford map but the street is not shown. The street appears on the 1868 map but is not named and the shipyard is again marked. The street is called Monroe Place on a 1902 survey map. Ely Lane first appears in the 1904 city directory and is named for the Adrian Ely family.[128] He was the son of Dr. Calvin L. Ely, Branford's first dentist and a captain in the Civil War.

The end of Ely Street at the Branford River.

EMERSON DRIVE

Branford Hills
See The Greens

ENGLISH ROAD

Johnsons Point, off Wood Road and loops back

The street appears briefly as a named road in the 1960s. It is really a private drive to a few waterfront homes. The street was named for the English family of New Haven who for many years had summer homes at Johnsons Point.

ESTHER PLACE

Branford Point, off Harborview Avenue to a dead end
Map #1941 land of Margaret W. Montelius

The street first appears in the 1942 city directory and is named for Esther Ely who had a summer home "The Pines" on Goodsell Point.

ETZEL ROAD

Pawson Park, off River Road to a dead end
Map #188 1930 land of Michael Etzel & Sons, Inc. at Pawson Park

The first house was built in 1904 but the street does not appear until the 1962 city directory. Some of Etzel Road and surrounding streets were developed by G.A.R. Hamre in 1916. The street is named for the Etzel family.

EUCLID STREET

Off Alps Road to Elinor Place, sometimes Euclid Avenue
Map #153 1928 property of George C. Kirkham and William R. Foote

The above property was subdivided into lots along Euclid Street, Elinor Place, and the southern portion of Alps Road. The street first appears on the 1953 Price & Lee map but was here earlier. A road connecting Elinor Place and Euclid Street was never completed and today is a right of way. Euclid was a Greek mathematician (3rd century B. C.) who developed the field of geometry. It is not known if that is the origin of this street name.

The Streets, Alphabetical

EVERGREEN PLACE

Off West End Avenue to a dead end, sometimes Evergreen Road
Map #472 1951 proposed street, land of the Malleable Iron Fittings Co.
Map #755 1959 Evergreen Place to the Town of Branford as a public highway

The street first appears on the 1953 Price & Lee map and was accepted as a town road in 1962.[129]

FAIRLAWN AVENUE

Indian Neck, off Indian Neck Avenue to a dead end
Map #73 1918 Branford Gardens, owned and developed by John J. Linsky of Naugatuck

The street was accepted as a town road in 1935[130] from John J. Linsky and first appears in the 1936 city directory. It was part of the Branford Gardens development.

FAIRLAWN AVENUE

Stony Creek
See Prospect Hill

FAIRVIEW AVENUE

Stony Creek
See Flying Point Road

FAIRVIEW TERRACE

Branford Hills
See Lakeview Terrace

FARM RIVER ROAD

Branford Hills
See Alex-Warfield Road

FARM RIVER ROAD

Short Beach, off Clark Avenue to a dead end
Map #351 1918 proposed building lots offered by Truman H. Bristol at Short Beach

The street was developed in 1918 and was originally named Bristol Lane for Short Beach land owner Harrison Bristol and his brother Truman. The street was accepted as a town road in 1930[131] when "all roads in Short Beach used by the public" were accepted as town roads. The street name was changed in 1958[132] because there was already a Bristol Street in Short Beach.

FARMINGTON AVENUE

Branford Hills
See Jefferson Road

FARVIEW DRIVE

Brushy Plain

The street originates in North Branford off Totoket Road and crosses slightly over the Branford border. The street first appears on the 1965 Price & Lee map.

FEATHERBED LANE

Damascus, off Damascus Road to East Main Street

The street was put through about 1840 when Benjamin Rogers built a house at 52 Featherbed Lane and the road appears on the 1868 map connecting Damascus to the Guilford Road (East Main Street). Another early settler was John Bishop of 34 Featherbed Lane. It appears as Totoket Road on 20th century maps and the name was changed about 1948 though it was locally long known as Featherbed Lane. According to tradition, when John Bishop moved here about 1843, a tree limb tore open a mattress scattering the feathers stuffed inside. Part of the street was developed by the A. M. Young Company.

FENWAY ROAD

Indian Neck, off Pawson Road to Sunset Manor Road
Map #99 1924 land of Indian Neck Land Co., 24 lots
Map #111 1924 Sunset Manor development

The street was part of the Sunset Manor development and was first named Ridge Road or Ridge Lane but does not appear until the 1936 Price & Lee map. The street name was changed in 1958[133] because there was already a Ridge Road in Stony Creek. The street was a private road owned by the First Ecclesiastical Society and was accepted as a town road in 1968.[134] Like the park and baseball stadium in Boston, it is probably named for "fen," an area of low, flat, marshy land.

FERN COURT

Mill Plain, off Debra Lane to a dead end
Map #950 1966 Brookhills West development

The street was accepted as a town road in 1971[135] and first appears in the 1976 city directory.

FERRY LANE

Pawson Park, off Spring Cove Road in both directions to dead ends
Map #705 1950 property of the First Ecclesiastical Society

The street first appears on the 1953 Price & Lee map, but cottages were built in the 1920s. When Pawson Park was a summer picnic area, steamers from New Haven brought passengers to Pawson Park and the Montowese House. The end of the street is called Ferry Path on some maps. The street was a private road owned by the First Ecclesiastical Society and was accepted as a town road in 1968.[136]

FIELD PLACE

Indian Neck, off South Montowese Street to Field Road
Map #473 1950 portion of land of G. Irving Field, proposed streets

The street was accepted as a town road in 1955[137] from G. Irving Field and first appears in the 1956 city directory. See also Barker Place and Field Road.

FIELD ROAD

Indian Neck, off Indian Neck Avenue to Field Place
Map #473 1950 portion of land of G. Irving Field, proposed streets

The street was accepted as a town road in 1951[138] from G. Irving Field and first appears in the 1953 city directory. See also Barker Place and Field Place.

FIFTH AVENUE

See Hotchkiss Grove

FIR TREE DRIVE

Off Pine Tree Drive to a dead end

The street was accepted as a town road in 1969[139] and first appears in the 1970 city directory as part of The Pines subdivision.

FIRST AVENUE

See Hotchkiss Grove

FIRST STREET

Branford Hills
See Bellview Road

FIRST STREET

Indian Neck
See Maltby Street

FLAT ROCK ROAD

Stony Creek
See Leetes Island Road-Paved Street

FLAT ROCK ROAD

Stony Creek, off Leetes Island Road south to the intersection of Flat Rock Road Extension and Old New England Road, sometimes Old Flat Rock Road, High Rock Road

The street was accepted as a town road in 1921[140] from Mary Perricone, Stephen O. Tucker and others. The street was here by 1750 when the house (still standing) at 29 Flat Rock Road was built. The "flat rock" is actually on Leetes Island Road opposite the entrance to Flat Rock Road[141] and was called High Rock Road by the locals.[142] Land at flat rock appears in the town records in 1754.[143] The southern portion was renamed Flat Rock Road Extension much later. There were several developments during the 20th century including Valley Acres in 1977.

FLAT ROCK ROAD EXTENSION

Stony Creek, off Flat Rock Road to Leetes Island Road

This portion of Flat Rock Road appears on the 1868 map. The name Flat Rock Road Extension first appears in the 1974 city directory and was accepted as a town road the same year.[144]

FLAX MILL ROAD

Mill Plain, off Northford Road and becomes Thompson Road, sometimes Flaxseed Lane
Maps #1114 & #1028 1967 Flax Mill Road, Wildmere subdivision

The street appears on the 1868 Beers map. It was a right of way or path off North Branford Road where a flax mill once stood[145] and the path went through to Mill Plain. Flax grew well in Branford and was used to make linen. The street was developed in the mid to late 20th century with several subdivisions and an industrial area along Route 139. The street was accepted as a town road in 1974.[146] The southern part of Flax Mill Road was renamed Thompson Road in 1975 for the Henry G. Thompson Company.

FLORENCE ROAD

Branford Hills, off Alps Road to Jefferson Road
Map #780 1958 owner & developer Mitchell & Florence Keszychi

The street was accepted as a town road in 1958[147] from Mitchell Keszychi and first appears in the 1960 city directory and was named for one of the owners. The town initially refused to accept the road due to its condition.[148] The street was later extended from Alps Road through to Jefferson Road[149] and an extension connected to Orchard Hill Road was accepted in 1971.[150]

FLYING POINT ROAD

Stony Creek, west from the junction of Thimble Islands Road and Prospect Hill Road to a dead end, sometimes Fairview Avenue, Flying Point Avenue, see also Thimble Islands Road

The road west of Prospect Hill Road along the water was built in 1869[151] and was referred to as Fairview Avenue until 1922. Flying Point Road, more commonly referred to as Flying Point Avenue from the 1870s until 1942 was from Main Street to Flying Point (now Thimble Islands Road). That is, it was the road past the Chapin water fountain, in front of Seaside Hall south to the water. Sometimes the entire main road in Stony Creek from the railroad underpass to Flying Point was called Flying Point Avenue. Map #539 refers to the portion toward Prospect Hill as Lake Street.

The current designation of Flying Point Road was first used in the 1928 city directory as that road west of Prospect Hill Road along the water to the end of Flying Point. After 1928 some of the maps still refer to it as Fairview Avenue. The origin of the name Flying Point is not known. The street is in the National Register Stony Creek Historic District.

FOREST STREET

Granite Bay, off Grove Street to Union Street, sometimes Forest Avenue or Road, see Edgewood Road
Map #24 1906 proposed new highway at Short Beach

The street was built in 1906 and was accepted as a town road the same year.[152] It does not appear on maps or directories until the 1930s. The northern part of Granite Bay was heavily forested and before the area was developed there was a small commercial wood cutting operation.

FOREST STREET EXTENSION

Granite Bay, off Forest Street to Hill Street, sometimes Klondike Road

The street first appears on the 1965 Price & Lee map, but the houses were built much earlier. This northern section of Granite Bay was called Klondike due to its remoteness. The roads in "Klondike" were built by the town between 1910 and 1912.[153]

Flying Point Road and Prospect Hill. Photo postcard by Edward W. Quimby.

Main Street in 1950 showing the stores in Fourth Ward. Photo by Earl Colter.

FOURTH AVENUE

See Hotchkiss Grove

FOURTH WARD

Fourth Ward is a section of Branford just west of Branford Center and first appears in 1650 as the Quarter or Quarter District.[154]

FRANK STREET

Indian Neck, off Indian Neck Avenue to Quarry Dock Road,
 sometimes Roden or Rodden Road
Maps #344 & #459 1945 land of Malleable Iron Fittings Co.

The street appears on the 1905 Bird's-Eye view map but as a dead end. It was built through to other streets and developed further in the late 1940s. The street appears on the 1924 Sanborn map as Roden Road[155] parenthesis Frank Street. The connection to the name Frank was not determined.

GARDEN STREET

Indian Neck, off Indian Neck Avenue to a dead end
*Map #73 1918 Branford Gardens, owned and developed
 by John J. Linsky, 68 lots*

The street was accepted as a town road in 1935[156] from John J. Linsky and first appears in the 1936 city directory. It was part of the Branford Gardens development.

GEORGE STREET

Indian Neck, off Fairlawn Avenue to a dead end
*Map #73 1918 Branford Gardens, owned and developed
 by John J. Linsky, 68 lots*

The street was accepted as a town road in 1935[157] from John J. Linsky as part of the Branford Gardens development and first appears in the 1936 city directory. It was originally named Highland Avenue and the street name was changed in 1958[158] because there was already a Highland Avenue in Short Beach.

GENTILE PLACE

Branford Hills, off West Main Street to Donna Lane
Map #496 1952 land of Anthony Gentile

The street first appears on the 1950 Price & Lee map and is named for the Gentile family. It was originally a dead end and was later connected to other streets as they were developed.

GILBERT LANE

Branford Hills, off West Main Street to Donna Lane,
   sometimes Gilbert Drive

The street was accepted as a town road in 1948[159] from the A. C. Gilbert Company and first appears on the 1953 Price & Lee map. The A. C. Gilbert Company of New Haven built Plant B on West Main Street about 1945 to manufacture products for World War II. The plant manufactured motors for Erector sets, transformers for American Flyer trains, and other products.[160]

GLEN STREET

Short Beach, off Shore Drive to a dead end
Map #66 & #94 1910 property of Edward B. Knowles

The street was developed in 1910 with lots sold by Edward B. Knowles but does not appear on the Price & Lee maps until 1959. Most of the original plan never materialized and included another street called Oak Street. Glen Street was accepted as a town road in 1930[161] when "all roads in Short Beach used by the public" were accepted as town roads.

GLENDALE COURT

Blackstone Acres
See Rocky Ledge Lane

GLENDALE PLACE

Short Beach, off Westwood Road to a dead end, sometimes
   Glenwood Avenue
Map #99 1922 property of William J. Kennedy, lots on Glendale
   Place & others

The street first appears on the 1924 Sanborn map. The street was accepted as a town road in 1930[162] when "all roads in Short Beach used by the public" were accepted as town roads.

GOAT ALLEY

Branford Hills, off Matthew Road to Brainerd Road

The street appears as a twenty-foot road or driveway on the 1926 development plan for Montvale but is not named. Today it is a right of way parallel to West Main Street connecting Brainerd Road and Matthew Road and has a street sign. It does not appear in the city directories or maps except online on Google maps. It is not an official town road and the houses facing it have a West Main Street address.

GOLDSMITH ROAD

Off East Main Street, becomes Towner Swamp Road

This street is near the Branford-Guilford border and is not shown on most Branford maps. The northern portion first appears on the 1950 Price & Lee map as Orchard Lane and Towner Swamp Road is on the 1954 zoning map. The road appears on the 1868 Beers map for Guilford and is named for the Goldsmith family of that town who had houses just east of the end of the road.

GOODSELL POINT ROAD

Branford Point, off Harbor Street to a dead end,
   sometimes Goodsell Road

Goodsell Point Road first appears on the 1868 Beers map. It is named for Thomas Goodsell who came to Branford in 1670 and purchased four acres at Mulliners Neck. The road was sometimes called Shepard Road for the family who lived at 99 Harbor Street.[163] An extension of Goodsell Point Road was accepted as a town road in

1945[164] from Edith (Stannard) Johnson. The intersection of Harbor Street, Goodsell Point Road, and Stannard Avenue was called Four Corners or Buckley Corner.

GOULD LANE

From Featherbed Lane to Leetes Island Road

The street appears on the 1868 Beers map connecting Featherbed Lane with Leetes Island Road (Paved Street) and living on the street was Elias Gould. The Gould family owned property in this area by the mid-1700s. The western part was later developed by the A. M. Young Company and more homes were built along the eastern end of Gould Lane in 2000.

GOVERNORS ISLAND

Stony Creek
See Central Avenue

GRANITE BAY

See Batrow Lane, Burr Street, Edgewood Road, Forest Street and Extension, Grove Street, Hill Street, Sherwood Street, Stone Street, and Union Street.

Granite Bay is a section of Short Beach north of Shore Drive that was settled in the early 1900s as a year-round community. The northern part of Granite Bay was called Klondike because it was densely wooded and out of the way.

GRANITE ROAD

Stony Creek, off Red Hill Road and becomes Ashman Court
Map #1225 1974 Red Hill Estates development

The street first appears in the 1977 city directory and was accepted as a town road the same year.[165] It is named for the stone that was quarried here.

GRAY LEDGE ROAD

Short Beach, off Shore Drive to a dead end, sometimes Greyledge Road

This road leads to three houses; the first was the "Gray Ledge" cottage built about 1910. The street first appears in the 1960 city directory and does not appear on any town map until 1986 (Beazley Company Realty map).

GRAYS LANE

Stony Creek
See Sachem Road

GREENFIELD AVENUE

Cherry Hill, off Cherry Hill Road to Avon Road
Maps #670 & #765 1957 part of the Cherry Hill Estates

The street first appears in the 1959 city directory.

The Granite Bay Hotel at the corner of Main Street (now Shore Drive) and Grove Street.

The Streets, Alphabetical 81

GREENFIELD TERRACE

Blackstone Acres
See Hawthorne Terrace

GREENWICH-KILLINGLY EXPRESSWAY

See Connecticut Turnpike

GRIFFING POND ROAD

Damascus, off Damascus Road to Sunset Hill Drive
Maps #409 1948 and #679 1957 layout of Griffing Pond Road, Sunset Hill Drive and Meadow Wood Road by the A. M. Young Company

The street was accepted as a town road in 1948[166] from the A. M. Young Co. and first appears in the 1950 city directory. The street is not on the 1868 map. Lewis Griffing came to Branford about 1875 and married Emily Bush of Pleasant Point. The property was later owned by their son Homer Griffing.

GROVE AVENUE

Pine Orchard, off Pine Orchard Road to Pasadena Road
Map #23 1907 Blackstone Park owned by F. C. Bradley

The street was developed and lots sold by Frederick C. Bradley in 1908 as part of Blackstone Park. The street name appears on the 1924 Sanborn map. A proposal to change the street name to Lathrop Road in 1958 was rejected.[167] The street is named for the grove of trees at the triangle of Pine Orchard Road and Spring Rock Road where people used to picnic and for which Pine Orchard is named.

GROVE PLACE OR STREET

Indian Neck
See Cottage Street

GROVE STREET

Granite Bay, off Shore Drive to Hill Street, sometimes Grove Street Extension is mentioned
Map #24 1906 lay out of Grove and Forest Streets

This street is the entrance to the Granite Bay section of Branford and was developed when Edgar Forbes began selling lots in 1902. The street was built by the town in 1905 and was accepted as a town road the same year.[168]

GUILFORD ROAD OR TURNPIKE

See also East Main Street, Boston Post Road, Leetes Island Road

The Guilford Turnpike was the portion of East Main Street from North Branford Road east to the Guilford line. Guilford Road at times referred to both the eastern portion of East Main Street and the eastern portion of Leetes Island Road.

HALLS POINT ROAD

Stony Creek, off Thimble Islands Road to a dead end, sometimes West Avenue, locally called **Dog Alley**, see also West Point Road

Halls Point Road was put through in the mid-18th century when several houses were built. The 1924 Sanborn map marks the road "Halls Point Road (West Avenue)." The street was called West Avenue in the city directories from 1897 until 1926. From 1928 until 1942 it is called West Point Road. Starting in the 1946 city directory the road is designated as Halls Point Road and is named for the Alanson Hall family. Alanson Hall came to Branford in 1829 when he married Rebecca Walker of Damascus. The Flats is the mud between Halls Point and the main beach on Thimble Islands Road. The street is in the National Register Stony Creek Historic District.

HALSTEAD LANE

Pine Orchard, off Pine Orchard Road to a dead end

The street was originally called Maple Avenue then Linden Avenue and houses were built about 1900. More lots were sold by Frederick C. Bradley in 1916. The street name was changed in 1958[169] because there was already a Linden Avenue in Indian Neck. It is probably named for R. Halstead Mills who lived on the street.[170]

The Streets, Alphabetical 83

Aerial of Halls Point Road taken by Earl Colter in 1987.

Halstead Lane in Pine Orchard was formerly called Linden Avenue.

HAMMER PLACE

Branford Center, off Kirkham Street to a dead end

The street was developed in 1942 and was deeded to the town in 1947[171] by William Meffert, Jr. It is named for the Hammer family, owners of the Malleable Iron Fittings Company. Alfred Hammer's estate "Elverhoi" stood on this property and some of the stone walls from the estate are still along the street.

HAMRE LANE

Branford Center, off East Main Street to a dead end

The street was originally named Beach Street and first appears on the 1914 Sanborn map as an unnamed driveway and as Beach Street on the 1929 Sperry map. In 1923 lots were sold by G.A.R. Hamre to Mike Petela, John A. Johnson, and Charles Estrom. It was accepted as a town road in 1941[172] from Hamre. The street name was changed in 1958[173] to Jerry's Island Road but was revoked a month later in favor of Hamre Lane. It was named for Gustave A.R. Hamre, a native of Norway and local businessman, who lived at 26 East Main Street. His wife was Estelle Beach.

HARBOR STREET

Branford Point, off West End Avenue south to a dead end,
   sometimes Branford Point Road, Point Road
See also North Harbor Street

The southern portion of Harbor Street was built by the mid-18th century and much of the land was owned by the Obed Linsley family. Access to Goodsell Point and the harbor was via Stannard Avenue until a bridge was built across the Mill Creek in 1820 and the road north of the creek was built. This northern portion of Harbor Street was sometimes referred to as Branford Point Road. The road north of Maple Street currently part of Harbor Street was called Double Beach Road from 1897 to 1926. The street is in the National Register Branford Point Historic District.

The Streets, Alphabetical 85

HARBORVIEW AVENUE

Branford Point, off Goodsell Point Road to Esther Place,
   sometimes Harbor View
Map #264 1941 property of Margaret Montelius

The street first appears in the 1942 city directory.

HARBOUR VILLAGE

Off Short Beach Road and exits via Cider Mill Lane to Stannard Avenue
Map #1057 1969 Harbour Village, also known as Bay Colony

Harbour Village is a condominium development built in 1969 in several phases. The condominiums have a Harbour Village address.

HARDING AVENUE

Indian Neck, off Indian Neck Avenue to a dead end
Map #219 1925 layout of Harding Avenue

The street first appears in the 1897 city directory and lots were sold over the next decade. The road was accepted as a town road in 1925[174] and is named for Michael P. Harding of 116 Montowese Street. Michael Harding was born in 1850, said to be the first Irish child born in Branford.

HARRISON AVENUE

Branford Center, off Main Street to Rose Street,
   sometimes Harrison Street

The street first appears in the 1895 city directory and was extended in 1897.[175] Captain Farrington Harrison's house stood at 960 Main Street and was torn down in 1950. The street was developed by his grandson Henry G. Harrison. The street is in the National Register Branford Center Historic District. The Harrison family were among the first English settlers of Branford.

HARRISON STREET

Short Beach
See Valley Street

Harbor Street looking north toward Mill Creek. The Malleable Iron Fittings Company is in the background. Photo by Kathleen M. Seaburg.

Haycock Point

HART AVENUE

Pine Orchard, off Pine Orchard Road to Club Parkway,
   sometimes Hart Place

The street was developed in the early 1900s and appears on the 1924 Sanborn map as Hart Place. It is probably named for Harold Hart and family of Hartford, long-time Pine Orchard summer residents.

HAWTHORNE TERRACE

Blackstone Acres, from Riverside Drive to Woodvale Road,
   sometimes Hawthorne Avenue
Map #663 1956 Blackstone Acres

It was originally named Greenfield Terrace and first appears with that name on the 1960 Chamber of Commerce map. Hawthorne Terrace, formerly known as Greenfield Avenue, was accepted as a town road in 1960[176] from Sturgess & Jockmus, Inc.

HAYCOCK POINT EAST AND WEST

Indian Neck, off Limewood Avenue, sometimes East
   and West Avenue or Road
Map #56 1911 shore lots at Haycock Point, property of Richard and J. H. Bradley

Brothers Richard and J. Hubert Bradley, contractors from Branford Center, purchased about five acres from James and Harriet Palmer in 1894.[177] Haycock is named for the rock at the end of the point that looks like a haystack. The Bradleys built cottages for themselves and others throughout the early 1900s. The area was originally called Stony Hill or Brown Point. A 1928 map calls one of the roads Cinder Drive. The corner of Haycock Point East and Limewood Avenue was called Tryon's Corner.

HAYSTACK ROAD

Brushy Plain, off Rolling Hill Road to a dead end
Map #1377 1977 Laurel Hill, Phase 2

The street first appears in the 1978 city directory. The street was part of the Laurel Hill subdivision, owner and developer Herbert Small.

HAZEL DRIVE

Brushy Plain, off Brushy Plain Road to Millwood Road
Map #783 1960 Millwood development

The street was accepted as a town road in 1961[178] from Edward Waltman Associates, Inc. and first appears in the 1962 city directory.

HELEN ROAD

Branford Hills, off Burban Drive to a dead end
Map #1061 1970 distribution of a portion of property of Peter P. Donadio et al

The street was originally named Yale Road and first appears on the 1953 Price & Lee map. The street name was changed in 1958[179] because there was already a Yale Court in Short Beach. A connection to the name Helen was not made.[180]

HEMINGWAY STREET

Indian Neck, off Linden Avenue to Dorr Street
Map #302 1913 building lots Pawson Park Road at the corner of Linden Avenue

The street was developed in 1913 and was originally named Cedar Street.[181] The street name was changed in 1958[182] because there was already a Cedar Street in Branford Center. The name probably refers to Donald H. Hemingway who bought a cottage in 1925.[183] The street was a private road owned by the First Ecclesiastical Society and was accepted as a town road in 1968.[184]

HEMLOCK ROAD

Brushy Plain, off Brushy Plain Road to Hosley Avenue
Map #782 1959 Millwood subdivision, owner Branford Development Corp.

The street was accepted as a town road in 1961[185] from Edward Waltman Associates, Inc. and first appears the 1962 city directory.

HERITAGE HILL ROAD

Brushy Plain, off Brushy Plain Road to Side Hill Road,
   sometimes Heritage Road
Map #909 1966 Laurel Acres subdivision, owner and developer Gargano Construction Company.

The street first appears in the 1968 city directory and the street was developed by contractor Raymond J. Gargano of Branford.

HICKORY HILL LANE

Mill Plain, off Mill Plain Road to Huntington Drive,
   sometimes Hickory Hill Road
Map #1344 1976 Hickory Hill subdivision, property of Anthony Giordano

The street first appears in the 1981 city directory.

HICKORY ROAD

Indian Neck, off Frank Street to Oak Ridge Road,
   sometimes Hickory Oak Ridge
Map #459 1945 building lots, property of the Malleable Iron Fittings Co.

The street was accepted as a town road in 1949[186] from the Malleable Iron Fittings Company and first appears on the 1954 zoning map.

HIGH MEADOW ROAD

Brushy Plain, off Brushy Plain Road to Valley Brook Road
Map #863 1962 Cedar Heights subdivision, Paramont Building Company

The street first appears in the 1965 city directory and was accepted as a town road in 1969.[187] The developer was Vincent Pesce.[188]

HIGH PLAINS ROAD

Mill Plain, off Huntington Road to a dead end,
   sometimes High Plains Drive
Map #1048 1971 final plans for Huntington Ridge

The street first appears in the 1973 city directory and was accepted as a town road in 1974.[189]

HIGH ROCK ROAD

Stony Creek
See Flat Rock Road

HIGH SCHOOL AVENUE

Branford Center
See Laurel Street

HIGHLAND AVENUE

Short Beach, off Clark Avenue to a dead end, sometimes Highland Park, Court or Hill

The street was settled in the 1890s with summer cottages overlooking the Farm River.

HIGHLAND AVENUE

Indian Neck
See George Street

Hillside Avenue looking toward Main Street. Photo by Earl Colter.

HILL STREET

Granite Bay, Burr Street becomes Hill Street and loops
   back to Grove Street

The street was developed in the early 1900s. The city directories and Price & Lee maps do not list the streets in Granite Bay until 1928 and before that the residences are listed as Short Beach with no addresses. The street is on a hill, but the Hillman family also owned a house on the street. The northern part of Hill Street was referred to as Granite Bay Terrace.

HILLSIDE AVENUE

Branford Center, off Main Street to a dead end, sometimes
   Hillside Terrace

The street first appears on the 1856 map and is named for the Linsley house that sat atop the hill. The house was called "Hillside Place" and was torn down in 2012. The foot of the street toward Ivy Street was called Meadow Street. Part of the street was accepted as a town road in 1938[190] from Antonia Dombrowski. The street is in the National Register Branford Center Historic District.

HILLTOP DRIVE

Brushy Plain, off Brushy Plain Road to a dead end
Map #1111 1958 property of Philamonia Walston

The street first appears in the 1960 city directory.

HOADLEY ROAD

Branford Hills, off Matthew Road to Brainerd Road, sometimes
   Hoadley Place
Map #85 1926 Montvale, Lakeview Realty Co., owners Ideal Homes Co.
Map #363 1946 Montvale

The street was part of the Montvale development and first appears on the 1946 Price & Lee map as Hoadley Place. It is named for the Hoadley family, first settlers of Branford.

HOLLY LANE

Stony Creek, connects Sachem Road and Squaw Brook Road

The street first appears on the 1936 Price & Lee map but is not named. It was originally called Wallmo Road and may have been here earlier. Pere Wallmo lived here until his death in 1953. The name change is not among those officially accepted by the town in 1958, however, the name was changed about that time and first appears as Holly Lane in the 1960 city directory. The street is in the National Register Stony Creek Historic District.

HOME PLACE

Branford Center, off Main Street to a dead end
Map #59 1925 plan of Home Place, property of Thomas O'Brien
Map #491 1952 extension of Home Place from estate of Frank Maturo

The street first appears in the 1926 city directory and was accepted as a town road in 1937[191] from the estate of Thomas O'Brien, Jr. of 215 Main Street. The southern portion was developed in 1952. The street is in the National Register Canoe Brook Historic District. Thomas O'Brien came to Branford by 1900 from Norwich.

HOME PLACE

Hotchkiss Grove
See Orchard Avenue

HOME PLACE

Pine Orchard
See McLean Place

HOMESTEAD PLACE

Brushy Plain, off Brushy Plain Road to a dead end
Map #477 1948 layout of lots for Michael Struzinsky, new road

The street was accepted as a town road in 1952[192] from Kathleen (Barry) Struzinsky and first appears on the 1953 Price & Lee map. Alexander and Mary Stuzinski came to Branford about 1900.

HOPSON AVENUE
Branford Center, off Main Street to Meadow Street

The street first appears on the 1856 map and was owned and developed by Philander Hopson, a local contractor. Originally Hopson Avenue went to the train depot to a dead end until Meadow Street was built in 1894. In 1907 the town proposed to regrade the street and found it had never been accepted as a town road or the boundaries set which was done at that time.[193] The street is in the National Register Branford Center Historic District.

HOPYARD PLAIN

Hopyard was a section of Branford during the colonial period that first appears in the town records in 1682 "hop yard plaine."[194] It was sometimes called Hopping Plain and according to tradition there were extensive hop fields. The term was used into the 20th century. It is the area along North Branford Road (Route 139).

Aerial showing Hopson Avenue, Rogers Street, Meadow Street, and part of Hammer Field. Photo by Earl Colter.

HOSLEY AVENUE

Branford Hills, off West Main Street to Brushy Plain Road, sometimes Hosley Road, Saltonstall Road, Lake Road, East Haven Road

Loring D. Hosley purchased a farm near Lake Saltonstall in 1827, later owned by his son Benjamin A. Hosley and the road was called Saltonstall or Lake Road. Saltonstall Road appears to refer to the southern portion of today's Hosley Avenue and Lake Road the northern portion. On the 1856 map a small section of the road was on the southern end and another section on the northern end but the two sections were not connected. The Hosley farm was accessed via Cherry Hill Road. By 1868 the entire stretch of road along the lake was there connecting West Main Street with Brushy Plain Road. The Hosley and other farms were sold to the New Haven Water Company in the 1890s for the Lake Saltonstall reservoir. The upper portion of Hosley Avenue was a dirt road until the late 20th century. Hosley Avenue first appears as a street name in the 1895 city directory but Saltonstall Road was still referred to until 1932. The lake was originally called Furnace Pond and renamed for Rev. Gurdon

Early view of Hotchkiss Grove from First Avenue along Seaview Avenue.

Saltonstall (1666-1724) of New London who was the tenth governor of Connecticut. He was married to Elizabeth Rosewell of Branford and had a mansion on the lake.

HOTCHKISS GROVE

Map #22 1907 Hotchkiss Grove owned by Emerson M. Hotchkiss[195]
Map #152 1914 Hotchkiss Grove and Pine Orchard West

Hotchkiss Grove is a section of Branford originally part of Stony Hill Point. The area was settled about 1705 when John Blackstone built a farm house which still stands at 37 First Avenue. The house and 100 acres were purchased by Emerson M. Hotchkiss of Waterbury in 1886 for a planned summer cottage community with beach access for the cottages (Seaview Avenue). It is named for Hotchkiss and the grove of trees between 7th and 8th Avenues where the family picnicked. He began building cottages but sold the rights for the development to Frederick Averill in 1916. Some of the cottagers pitched tents before their cottages were built.

Most of the 1907 plan for the Grove was built with some variations. A new road called West Side Avenue was planned to run parallel and north of Hotchkiss Grove Road from 1st Avenue to 8th Avenue. This road was never built and was the approximate location of the shoreline trolley tracks. Between 1st Avenue and 4th Avenue was a road to be called East Side Avenue. Two other roads north of Hotchkiss Grove called Woodlawn Avenue and Meadow Avenue were never developed or were later abandoned. Today the portion of Route 146 along the Avenues is Hotchkiss Grove Road to 2nd Avenue and becomes Elizabeth Street east to Pine Orchard. The streets in Hotchkiss Grove are private roads.[196]

1st or First Avenue[197] - It was an existing road for the John Blackstone House. First Avenue was extended to Seaview Avenue as part of the 1907 plan.

2nd or Second Avenue - Second Avenue was part of the 1907 plan.

Terrace Avenue - This road was part of the 1907 plan connecting 2nd and 5th Avenues but was never built.

3rd or Third Avenue - This street was originally planned as a small road north of Hotchkiss Grove Road. Third Avenue first appears on the 1946 Price & Lee map.

4th or Fourth Avenue - Fourth Avenue was originally planned as coming off Terrace Avenue north to Hotchkiss Grove Road but instead was built going all the way to Seaview Avenue.

5th or Fifth Avenue - This street was part of the 1907 plan, a portion also planned for north of Hotchkiss Grove Road was never built.

6th or Sixth Avenue - Sixth Avenue was originally only planned for north of Hotchkiss Grove Road but was built through to Seaview Avenue. The northern portion became part of Seventh Avenue.

7th or Seventh Avenue - This street was part of the 1907 plan but did not include the portion north of Hotchkiss Grove Road (see 6th Avenue).

8th or Eighth Avenue - Eighth Avenue was part of the 1907 plan including the portion north of Hotchkiss Grove Road.

Orchard Avenue - This street first appears on the 1924 Sanborn map and was not part of the 1907 plan.

Seaview Avenue - This street was part of the original 1907 plan and was the main road along the beach.

HOTCHKISS GROVE ROAD
Off Pine Orchard Road to Route 146 at 2nd Avenue

The street appears on the 1852 map and was the only road to Pine Orchard for nearly two centuries to access the Blackstone houses at 86 Hotchkiss Grove Road and 37 First Avenue. For many years this area was called Blackstoneville. Hotchkiss Grove Road connecting Limewood Avenue to Pine Orchard was built in 1886 and named at that time. This section became part of the Connecticut State Highway system- Route 146 in 1955 and as part of the National Register Route 146 scenic highway in 1996.

HOWARD AVENUE

Brocketts Point, off Lanphiers Cove Road to a dead end,
  sometimes Howard Street
*Map #362 1946 & #399 1947 Lanphier Cove Woods, property of Grace
  LaBarron Lanphier*

The town accepted Howard Avenue at Lanphiers Cove in 1947[198] and the street first appears in the 1950 city directory. It is named for Howard Lanphier, husband of Grace. The portion ending in a dead end at the water was called Ridge Rock Road on an earlier map.

HOWD AVENUE

Stony Creek, off Leetes Island Road to Thimble Islands Road
*Map #495 1951 property of Earle R. Mann and Charles A. Howd,
  proposed street*

The street first appears in the 1950 city directory and was accepted as a town road in 1958[199] from Charles A. Howd. A portion of the road appears on the map as Atwater Extension but it appears this name was never adopted. A few houses were built in the late 1940s. It is named for the Howd family, among the first settlers of Stony Creek whose house still stands at 72 Thimble Islands Road.

HUDSON COURT

Indian Neck, off Linden Avenue to a dead end

The street was a private road leading to a log cabin built and owned by the Meffert family. The street appears on the 1924 Sanborn map as "Hudson Court or Meffert Road" and appears in the 1946 city directory as Hudson Court. The street is now an extension of Old Pawson Road and is vacant land. Part of Hudson Court became Old Pawson Road.

HUNTINGTON DRIVE

Mill Plain, off Mill Plain Road, becomes Hickory Hill Lane;
  sometimes Huntington Lane
Map #1048 1971 final plan Huntington Ridge

The street first appears in the 1973 city directory and was accepted as a town road in 1974 from Frederick Corbin.[200]

View from MIF showing Long Bridge over the river, the signal tower, and part of Terhune Avenue. Photo by Harry O. Andrews.

Aerial of the Indian Point Club.

INDIAN NECK

Indian Neck is a section of Branford which was originally the peninsula southwest of Sybil's Creek that was retained by the Totoket Indians. It is mentioned on the first page of the town records. It is now more loosely the section of town from the Branford River along Indian Neck Avenue, south and east to Hotchkiss Grove. Much of the peninsula became known as Pawson Park.

INDIAN NECK AVENUE

Indian Neck, from Maple Street to South Montowese Street

The street was developed in the 1880s.[201] The western portion of Indian Neck Avenue and its side streets were settled by Scandinavians who worked at the Malleable Iron Fittings Company. The entrance off Maple Street was reconfigured in 2006.

INDIAN NECK ROAD

See South Montowese Street

INDIAN POINT ROAD

Stony Creek, off Thimble Islands Road to a dead end at the public dock, sometimes Public Dock Road

Ebenezer Coe of Middlefield built the Indian Point House in 1854 and the road appears on the 1868 Beers map. In 1900 the old highway at Indian Point was abandoned and a new one built including a new dock area.[202] The Indian Point House was torn down after a 1965 fire destroyed the building. Subsequently a private beach club and restaurant were on the site and today is a private home.

INDIAN WOODS ROAD

Off Arrowhead Lane to Deer Path Road
Map #1164 1973 Indian Woods subdivision owned and developed by Ramzey Associates

The street first appears in the 1974 city directory. The development includes Arrowhead Lane, Deer Path Road, Indian Woods Road, and Soffer Place and was built in phases.

ISABEL LANE

Indian Neck, off South Montowese Street to Newton Road

The street first appears on the 1954 zoning map as Palmer Heights Road though the lone house on the street was built in 1930. James Palmer (1868-1956) owned large parcels of land on both sides of South Montowese Street and his wife Susan operated Palmer's Casino on Limewood Avenue. The street name was changed in 1958[203] because there was already a Palmer Road in Branford Center. The house was owned for many years by the Hanniford-Corcoran family and was named for Isabel Corcoran.

ISLAND VIEW AVENUE

Pine Orchard, off Lake Avenue along the water to a dead end,
  sometimes Great Plain Road, Pierpont Road, Wallace Avenue
Old Map #7 1893 property of Robert Wallace

Island View Avenue was the second area of Pine Orchard to be settled. Jared Pierpont built a farm house at Great Plain between 1856 and 1860. The road was built by the town in 1876[204] and called Great Plain Road. Pierpont died in 1872 and Robert Wallace of Meriden purchased the property. Wallace was the first person to make silver plate products in the country. The land was subdivided by 1880 and lots sold. After Wallace's death more lots were sold by real estate agent Frederick C. Bradley. The street was called Wallace Avenue and first appears on the 1924 Sanborn map as Island View.

IVY STREET

Branford Center, from Main Street to Brushy Plain Road

Ivy Swamp is mentioned in the town records in 1796[205] and the street appears on the 1852 map. In recent years, the portion from North Main Street to Brushy Plain Road is sometimes called North Ivy Street and has a street sign with N. Ivy St. The name is not officially used by the town. Part of Ivy Street was realigned and reconstructed in 1961.[206] A portion of the street is in the National Register Branford Center Historic District.

The Streets, Alphabetical

Island View Avenue looking east about 1905.

Ivy Street in the 1950s. Photo by Earl Colter

JACKSON DRIVE

Branford Hills, off West Main Street to Hosley Avenue

The street first appears on the 1930 Price & Lee map without a name and is named in the 1962 city directory. It was probably there when the Saltonstall School was built in 1912. A correlation to the name Jackson was not made.

JEFFERSON PLACE

Short Beach, off Shore Drive to a dead end

The street was put through about 1925 when several cottages were built and first appears in the 1928 city directory. It is named for Thomas S. W. and Thankful Jefferson who had a cottage on the street. The street was accepted as a town road in 1930[207] when "all roads in Short Beach used by the public" were accepted as town roads. Map #176 refers to Owens Place, a new road along the Farm River roughly parallel with Jefferson Place with four new lots. That road was never built.

Aerial postcard of Johnson Point showing the former Winchester-Bennett summer home.

JEFFERSON ROAD

Branford Hills, off West Main Street to Burban Drive
*Map #58 1912 Plan layout William S. Chidsey, Horace L. Chidsey
and William H. Hosley*

The northern portion of the street off West Main Street first appears on a 1912 map as Farmington Avenue and subsequently is called both Farmington Avenue and Jefferson Road. From 1939 until 1953 it is listed on maps as Farmington Avenue and in 1959 back to Jefferson Road when it first appears going through to Burban Drive. In 1955 this southern portion of Jefferson Road is called "a new road."[208] The Jefferson Woods condominiums were built starting in 1973 by Associated Builders Corporation.[209] The street is named for Thomas Jefferson, and connecting to it is Monticello Avenue.

JEFFREY LANE

Mill Plain, off Deforest Drive to a dead end
*Maps #582 & 606 1956 Cedar Lake Acres subdivision, owner
and developer Cedar Lake Construction Company*

The street was accepted as a town road in 1958[210] from Cedar Lakes Construction Company and first appears in the 1963 city directory. The origin of the name Jeffrey was not determined.

JOHN STREET

Branford, off Main Street to a dead end

The street was established about 1897 when John Donnelly, the village blacksmith, built his house and it appears on the 1905 Bird's-Eye view map. The street is in the National Register Branford Center Historic District. John Donnelly, a native of Ireland, came to Branford in 1889 from New Britain.

JOHNSONS POINT ROAD

Off Double Beach Road to a dead end, see Bennett Road
*Map #49 1911 property belonging to the heirs of Samuel Foote, 6 lots
Map #97 1919 building lots at Johnsons Point, owner William R. Foote*

Johnsons Point appears on the 1791 William Blodget map and was originally called Town Neck. The property was subdivided in 1902 by William R. Foote for an upscale summer community. The roads in Johnsons Point do not appear on maps until the 1960s. Nathaniel Johnson came to Branford in 1700 from Woodstock, Connecticut and the family owned this property by 1750.

JOURDAN ROAD

Branford Point, off Linsley Street to a dead end, sometimes Jourdan Drive
Map #689 1958 Jourdan Farm, Section D

The street was accepted as a town road in 1959[211] from Fannie Jourdan et al and first appears in the 1962 city directory. Frederick Jourdan, a native of Switzerland, came to Branford in 1850 and married Fannie E. Linsley of Branford Point (see Linsley Street). The Linsley farm became known as the Jourdan Farm. In 1876 he established the Jourdan Coal & Lumber Company at Dutch Wharf.

JUNIPER POINT ROAD

Pine Orchard, off Totoket Road to a dead end, sometimes Juniper Road

A house, known as the old red house, was built about 1735 which was accessed by a narrow dirt road (Juniper Point Road). Henry Rowe of New Haven purchased the point in 1902 and it was owned by the family for nearly a century. The street was developed from 1991 until 1996 as the Juniper Point subdivision.

KENYON STREET

Branford Hills, off West Main Street to a dead end
Map #85 1926 Montvale, Lakeview Realty Co., owners Ideal Homes Co.

The street first appears on the 1930 Price & Lee map as part of the Montvale development.

KIDDS CAVE ROAD

Short Beach, off Midwood Road to a dead end, sometimes Kid's or Kidd's
Map #1544 1977 Kidd's Cave subdivision, owner and developer Arnold T. Peterson

The street first appears in the 1981 city directory and is named for a nearby cave. It is a private road.

KILLAMS POINT ROAD

Off Shore Drive to a dead end
Map #80 1912 Killams Point lot plan

The area known as Town Meadows was leased by the First Ecclesiastical Society to Jay Russell in 1867 who in turn leased it to Henry Killam of New Haven in 1881. The Killam family built cottages and descendants still live here today. The First Ecclesiastical Society sold the land to the Killam-Murphy and other families in 1967 retaining 45 acres at the end known as Shepards Point. The street is a private road.

KING'S HIGHWAY

See Boston Post Road, East Main Street, Guilford Turnpike, Main Street, West Main Street

KIRKHAM STREET

Branford Center, off Main Street and becomes Maple Street

The street was put through between 1856 and 1868 and is named for William S. Kirkham one of the founders of a factory established in 1854 which became the Malleable Iron Fittings Company. The Kirkham Street bridge was built in 1894.

KLONDIKE

See Granite Bay

KNOLLWOOD DRIVE

Pine Orchard, off Pine Orchard Road and loops back
Map #790 1961 Knollwood subdivision owned and developed by Michael and Genevieve Giordano

The street was developed in phases on property originally owned by the A. M. Young Company and purchased by Giordano.[212] The street first appears on the 1964 Price & Lee map and was accepted as a town road in 1965[213] from Michael Giordano. Michael and Genevieve Giordano came to Branford about 1918.

Early 1900s view of the entrance to Killams Point.

Kirkham Street turning onto Main Street in the winter of 1934.

LAKE AVENUE

Pine Orchard, off Pine Orchard Road to Island View Avenue, sometimes Lake Place

The street first appears on the 1924 Sanborn map. Starting in 1930 it appears on the Price & Lee maps and city directories as Park Place then reappears in 1936 as Lake Avenue or sometimes Lake Place. The street was probably developed in the early 1900s when the English family had a summer cottage here. It is named for Mirror Lake which is nearby.

LAKE STREET

Stony Creek
See *Flying Point Road*

LAKESIDE DRIVE

Short Rocks
See *Stonegate Drive*

LAKEVIEW TERRACE

Branford Hills, off Rose Hill Road to a dead end
Map #446 1949 Pleasant View Homes development

The street was accepted as a town road in 1949[214] and was originally called Fairview Terrace. The name was changed in 1950[215] and the street first appears on the 1953 Price & Lee map.

LANPHIER PLACE

Branford Point
See *Lanphier Road*

LANPHIER ROAD

Branford Point, off Harbor Street to Stannard Avenue
Map #357 1947 property of Grace LeBarron Lanphier

The street was originally named Lanphier Road from Harbor Street west and the portion from Stannard Avenue to Lanphier Road called Lanphier Place. The streets were accepted as town roads in 1948[216] from Grace (LeBaron) Lanphier. The entire street became Lanphier

Road in 1958.[217] Horace Lanphier was the son of Olive Lanfare of Lanphiers Cove and built 136 Harbor Street about 1835.

LANPHIERS COVE

Lanphiers Cove is a section of Branford settled by the Lanphier[218] family in the early 18th century. It refers to a section of town but also to the bay in the harbor.

LANPHIERS COVE ROAD

Double Beach, off Double Beach Road to a dead end

The Oliver Lanphier family was one of the first settlers of the western part of Branford and built a house here (14 Lanphier Cove Road) about 1785. The Lanphier and Linsley families at Double Beach and Lanphier Cove were the only families in the area for many decades. The Lanphier house was torn down in 2011.

LATHROP ROAD

Pine Orchard
See Grove Avenue

LAUREL ACRES

Brushy Plain
See Brookwood Drive, Heritage Hill Road, and Overland Court

LAUREL HILL ROAD

Brushy Plain, off Brushy Plain Road to Piscitello Drive
Map #65 1915 Laurel Hill Farm
Map #417 1948 extension of Laurel Hill Road
Map #1082 1972 Laurel Hill Road, Highland Park

The street appears on the 1868 Beers map and was farm land until the area was developed in several phases during the mid to late 20th century. The street was accepted as a town road in 1976.[219] Laurel Hill does not appear in early town records.

LAUREL ROAD

Brocketts Point
See Dogwood Drive and Rustic Road

LAUREL STREET

Branford Center, off Main Street to Cedar Street

The street appears on the 1852 Whiteford map and was probably put through about that time. It was also called High School Avenue when the former Laurel Street School was the high school from 1894 until 1928. The street is in the National Register Branford Center Historic District.

LAVASSA TERRACE

Stony Creek, off 297 Thimble Islands Road to a dead end

The Terrace appears on some maps during the 1960s to 1980s and is not an official town road. Several cottages on Cedar Hill were built by Francis C. Bartholomew shortly after the Civil War and were purchased about 1920 by the Lavassa family.[220]

LAY-TOOLE AVENUE

Branford Center
See Park Place

LEETES ISLAND ROAD

Stony Creek, off East Main Street south to the junction of Stony Creek Road, continuing east to the Guilford line; also called Paved Street, Old Paved Street, Old Highway, Guilford Road
See Paved Street

The northern portion of Leetes Island Road from East Main Street south to Thimble Islands Road was put through in the late 18th century and was called Paved Street, a term still used by older residents. This portion of Leetes Island Road became a state road in 1906.[221]

The eastern portion from Stony Creek Road east to the Guilford line was put through by the mid-18th century and was the shore route to Guilford. This portion was called Leetes Island Road or Guilford Road. Until 1945 a small section from Stony Creek Road to School Street was called Northam Street, named for the Palmer-Northam family who owned 400 Leetes Island Road. This eastern section of Leetes Island Road became part of the Connecticut State Highway- Route 146 in 1933[222] and as part of the Route 146 National Register scenic highway in 1996.

The entire road from East Main Street south to the Guilford line was renamed Leetes Island Road in 1958.[223] A portion of the street is in the National Register Stony Creek Historic District.

LIMEWOOD AVENUE

Indian Neck, from Sybil Avenue to Hotchkiss Grove Road, part of scenic
  Route 146, sometimes Indian Neck Road, Limewood Grove Road

The street was put through by 1880 and was a summer resort destination with several hotels and summer cottages. The road was also referred to as Indian Neck Road.[224] Limewood Avenue became part of the Connecticut State Highway- Route 146 in 1955 and as part of the National Register Route 146 scenic highway in 1996. The beach along the street is called Limewood Beach, Limewood Grove or Scum Beach.

A small road north of Limewood Avenue and opposite West Haycock Point Road appears on the 1924 Sanborn map as Palmer Avenue and the houses today have a Limewood Avenue address. A small road west of 86 Limewood Avenue has an old wood sign "Edgelawn Avenue." There are a few cottages facing this driveway that also have a Limewod Avenue address. There are several places along Limewood Avenue where there are cottages tucked in the back. Another example is a driveway to the west of 70 Limewood Avenue.

The lime or limewood tree (not the citrus variety) is of the genus Tilia. Other names for the tree include Linden and Basswood (see the streets named Linden).

LINCOLN AVENUE

Branford Center, off Main Street to Cherry Street, sometimes
  Lincoln Street
*Map #96 1922 property of C. F. Mory and F. M. Hollweg,
  lots on Lincoln Avenue*

The street first appears in the 1925 city directory and was accepted as a town road in 1930.[225] It is presumed named for Abraham Lincoln.

The Streets, Alphabetical

Limewood Avenue looking east toward Haycock Point., The Montasco Inn is on the far right. Photo by John H. Morton

Looking west along Limewood Avenue. The Dairy J is on the left and the Waverly Hotel on the far right. Photo by Earl Colter.

LINDEN AVENUE

Indian Neck
See South Montowese Street

LINDEN AVENUE

Indian Neck, sometimes Lower Montowese Street

Linden Avenue is the shore route to the Pawson Park area of Branford; originally where the Totoket Indians lived after the English settlers came in 1644. The street probably follows an Indian path. The street was improved by the early 1800s when a few year-round houses were built. On the 1868 map the road extends slightly west of today's Owenego (40 Linden Avenue) and was extended west by Samuel Beach shortly afterwards. The street was a private road owned by the First Ecclesiastical Society and a portion in front of the Montowese House was accepted as a town road after the road caved in during the 1938 hurricane.[226] Another portion at the junction of Sybil Avenue to the current Indian Neck Fire Department was accepted in 1941[227] from Laura Wilford Ayer. The rest of the street was accepted as a town road in 1968.[228] A proposed road to the rear of the Montowese House to bypass Linden Avenue was proposed several times but was never approved.

LINDEN AVENUE

Pine Orchard
See Halstead Lane

LINDEN POINT ROAD

Stony Creek, off Thimble Islands Road south to the water, sometimes Linden Point Avenue

The street was put through about 1875 and the town surveyed the road in 1882.[229] Oliver B. Beach deeded a portion of the road to the town in 1941.[230] It is another Branford street named for the Linden tree. The street is in the National Register Stony Creek Historic District.

Linden Avenue was damaged in front of the Montowese House during the Hurricane of 1938. Photo by Donald F. Higney.

Linden Point Road in Stony Creek looking south toward the water.

LINSLEY STREET

Branford Point, off Maple Street to Stannard Avenue, sometimes
   Linsley Road, Castle Rock Road, Lindsley Street
Map #439 & #468 1948 part of Maple Corners developed by Ray U. Plant

The street appears on the 1852 map off Bradley Street connecting to Stannard Avenue and leading to the Linsley-Jourdan farm. The farm was located where 25 Linsley Street is today. The street was accepted as a town road in 1949[231] from Ray U. Plant.

LITTLE BAY LANE

Short Beach, off Shore Drive to a dead end

One of the earliest residents of Short Beach was the Wallingford branch of the Oneida Community who had property on Little Bay Lane. The Wallingford Oneida Community disbanded in 1878 and sold their interests in Wallingford and Short Beach. The street was originally called Beach Street and the street name was changed in 1958[232] because there was already a Beach Street in Branford Center. The street was accepted as a town road in 1930[233] when "all roads in Short Beach used by the public" were accepted as town roads. The southern end of Little Bay Lane is called Stanley Point named for the family who have summered here for over 130 years. Walter H. Stanley, son of the founder of Stanley Works of New Britain, came to Short Beach about 1880. In 1903 he remarked that "he saw the place [Short Beach] grow from a wilderness to a flourishing resort."

LITTLE PLAIN ROAD

See Tabor Drive

Little Plain first appears in the town records in 1667, "a place commonly called little plaine."[234] It was a section of Branford east of the Montowese Street railroad underpass including the meadows.[235] Little Plain Road was used as a street name and renamed Tabor Drive in 1958.

LOCUST STREET

Brushy Plain, off Hemlock Road to Millwood Drive, sometimes
  Locust Road
Map #783 1960 Locust Street, Brushy Plain

The street was accepted as a town road in 1961[236] from Edward Waltman Associates, Inc. and first appears in the city directory in 1962.

LONG POINT ROAD

Stony Creek, off Thimble Islands Road to a dead end, sometimes
  Long Point Avenue

The street does not appear on the 1868 map but was constructed by 1880. After 1895 the end of the street was called Rand Point named for the Henry P. Rand family of Brooklyn, New York. The street is in the National Register Stony Creek Historic District.

LONGFELLOW DRIVE

Branford Hills
See The Greens

LOWER MONTOWESE STREET

Indian Neck
See Linden Avenue

MACLEAN PLACE

Pine Orchard, off Club Parkway to Island View Avenue,
  sometimes McLean

The street was here in the 1880s, originally named Home Place and appears on the 1924 Sanborn map with that name. The street name was changed in 1958[237] because there was already a Home Place in Branford Center. Both names refer to the MacLean family, postmasters of the Pine Orchard post office for sixty years.

MAIN ROAD

See East Main Street

MAIN STREET

Branford Center, sometimes Boston Post Road, King's Highway, Towne Street, Route 1, Route 1A

Main Street was one of two streets developed by the English settlers in 1644 and was called Towne Street. The settlers divided the land into "homelots" and built their homes along Main and Montowese Streets. Land was also divided outside the town center for pasture, meadow, and wood lots. The street was part of the lower Boston Post Road or King's Highway connecting New York City with Boston. The term Main Street is used on the 1868 map. Main Street became part of the Connecticut State Highway- Route 146 in 1955. The street is in the National Register Branford Center and Canoe Brook Historic Districts.

Main Street started at Bradley Street with lower house numbers starting at that intersection going east to the junction of Chestnut, Ivy, and East Main Street. The Blackstone Memorial Library was 134 Main Street. The street was redefined in 1958[238] as running from the railroad bridge rotary through Branford Center; that is from the

Main Street looking west from Chestnut Street. Photo by Earl Colter.

The Streets, Alphabetical

Phyllis Hibbard pretending she is fishing on Main Street in front of Bradley's Department Store. Photo by John H. Morton

Similar view of Main Street in 1952. Photo by Earl Colter

junction of the newly defined West Main Street at the railroad underpass to the junction of Ivy, Chestnut, and East Main Streets. The house numbers were changed at that time with the lowest numbers starting at the junction of Main, North Main, and West Main Streets. The Blackstone Library became 758 Main Street. The numbering of West Main Street was also changed.

MAIN STREET

Short Beach
See *Shore Drive*

MAIN STREET

Stony Creek
See *Thimble Islands Road*

MALTBY STREET

Indian Neck, off Pawson Road to Bayberry Lane
Map #302 1913 building lots Pawson Park Road at the corner
   of Linden Avenue

The street was developed in 1913 and was originally called 1st or First Street. The street name was changed in 1958[239] because there was already a First Avenue in Hotchkiss Grove. The street was a private road owned by the First Ecclesiastical Society and was accepted as a town road in 1968.[240] The street is named for Maltby Cove—William Maltby was a first settler of Branford and owned land at Indian Neck.

MANOR PLACE

Indian Neck, off Sunset Manor Road to Sunset Beach Road,
   sometimes Manor Road
Map #99 1924 land of Indian Neck Land Co., 24 lots
Map #111 1924 Sunset Manor development
Map #708 1950, received 1958 First Ecclesiastical Society

The street was part of the Sunset Manor development and first appears on the 1930 Price & Lee map but is not named. It was originally called Maple Lane. The street name was changed in 1958[241] because

The Streets, Alphabetical | 119

there was already a Maple Street in Branford Point. The street was a private road owned by the First Ecclesiastical Society and was accepted as a town road in 1968.[242]

MAPLE AVENUE

Pine Orchard
See Halstead Lane

MAPLE CORNERS

Branford Point
See Berry Patch Road, Linsley Street, Maple Street, Short Beach Road, and Swift Street

MAPLE HILL ROAD

Mill Plain
See Mill Plain Road, sometimes Maple Hill Queach Road

MAPLE LANE

Indian Neck
See Manor Place

MAPLE ROAD

Stony Creek
See Wallace Road

MAPLE STREET

Off Short Beach Road becoming Kirkham Street
Map #439 & #468 1948 land developed by Ray U. Plant as part of the Maple Corners

A road from Pages Point near the Railroad Depot to connect to the Dutch House Wharf was approved in 1855.[243] This is the eastern end of Maple Street from the former the Malleable Iron Fittings Company to today's Dutch Wharf Marina and the road appears on the 1868 map as Maple Street. The portion west of Harbor Street was laid out soon after[244] and was sometimes called Branford Point Road. Some of the eastern section was later developed by the Malleable Iron Fittings

Company and the western end was part of Maple Corners developed by Ray U. Plant in 1948. Portions of the street were widened and regraded in 1901, 1919, and 1928. Part of the street was accepted as a town road in 1942[245] and a portion in front of the MIF was abandoned in 1953.[246] The street is in the National Register Branford Point Historic District.

MARBAR STREET

Off North Branford Road (Route 139) to a dead end
Map #786 1959 owners Louis and Evelyn Desiderio

The ranch houses were built in 1961 by the P. J. Cricco Construction Company of New Haven and sold for $18,500.[247] The street was accepted as a town road in 1964[248] from Louis Desi and first appears in the city directory the same year. The land originally belonged to the Bartholomew family.

MARIAN ROAD

Branford Hills, off Alps Road to Eli Yale Terrace, sometimes Marion
Map #394 1946 & #385 1948 Ballou Heights, property of Raymond C. & Edith Y. Ballou shows Ballou Road, Yale Terrace and Marian Road

The street was accepted as a town road in 1949[249] and first appears in the 1950 city directory. The street was developed and lots sold by Raymond C. and Edith (Prout) Ballou of 32 Alps Road as part of Ballou Heights. Edith Ballou's mother was Marian (Yale) Prout.

MARINERS LANE

Stony Creek
See West Point Road

MARSHALL PLACE

Off Marshall Road to a dead end
Map #581 1955 Little Plain subdivision by Bradley, Enquist & Williams Co.

Marshall Place and Marshall Road first appear in the 1950 city directory and were both accepted as town roads in 1957[250] from Bradley, Enquist & Williams Company.

MARSHALL ROAD

Off Ark Road to a dead end
See Marshall Place

MARTONE DRIVE

Branford Center
See Valley Court

MATTHEW ROAD

Branford Hills, off West Main Street to a dead end
Map #85 1926 Montvale, Lakeview Realty Co., owners Ideal Homes Co.
Map #657 1956 Summit Gardens developed by Summit Garden Apartments

The street first appears on the 1936 Price & Lee map and was part of the Montvale development by Robert Rosenthal and Ideal Homes. The street was accepted by the town in 1938[251] from Lakeview Realty Company and the southern section was developed in 1956 as part of Summit Gardens. The origin of the name was not determined.

McDERMOTT DRIVE

Off North Branford Road (Route 139) to a dead end

Developed in 1965 by Robert McDermott and first appears in the 1974 city directory.

McKINNEL COURT

Branford Point, off Harbor Street to a dead end, sometimes MacKinnel
See Bellaire Place
Maps #372 & #376 1947 land of Abraham McKinnel, building lots & proposed road

The street was accepted as a town road in 1949[252] from Abraham P. McKinnel and first appears on the 1950 Price & Lee map. Abraham McKinnel purchased 139 Harbor Street in 1880 and farmed the rear of the property.

MEADOW CIRCLE ROAD

Damascus, off Windmill Hill and loops back
Map #380 1948 lots on Meadow Circle Road

The street was accepted as a town road in 1948[253] from the A. M. Young Company and first appears in the 1950 city directory.

MEADOW STREET

Branford Center, off Kirkham Street to Montowese Street

Originally Hopson Avenue and Rogers Street went south directly to the train depot in front of the Malleable Iron Fittings Company. Meadow Street does not appear on the 1881 Bird's-Eye view map nor are there any buildings except at the base of Hopson and Rogers. The laying of a highway "across the meadows to Church Street" was approved at a Town Meeting December 5, 1894.[254] Land was purchased from Henry Fowler and the road constructed by Michael Mason and John T. Sliney.[255] The street first appears in the 1897 directory from "Montowese Street west to Rogers." The street appears on the 1905

Meadow Street looking east before it was filled in for Hammer Field.

Bird's-Eye map going all the way through from Montowese Street to Kirkham Street on the north side of the railroad tracks and new buildings were constructed along the street. The portion from Rogers Street to Kirkham Street was sometimes called Railroad Avenue. The street is in the National Register Branford Center Historic District.

MEADOW STREET

Branford Center

There was another Meadow Street that was north and parallel to Main Street connecting Ivy Street and Hillside Avenue. The street does not appear on the 1852 map but is on the 1856 and 1868 maps. It still appears on the 1905 Bird's-Eye map but is not on the 1924 Sanborn or subsequent maps. The new entrance to Rose Street built off Ivy Street in 1987 correlates approximately with the old Meadow Street.

MEADOW WOOD ROAD

Pine Orchard, off Griffing Pond Road to Sunset Hill Drive
Map #679 1957 road layout of Sunset Hill, Griffing Pond, and Meadow Wood Roads by the A. M. Young Company

The street was accepted as a town road in 1957[256] from the A. M. Young Company and first appears on the 1959 Price & Lee map. A proposal to change the name in 1958[257] to Deepwood Road was rejected.

MEDLEY LANE

Off Featherbed Lane to a dead end
Map #531 & #557 1954 property of Ben Medley, owned and developer

The street was accepted as a town road in 1956[258] from Benjamin S. and Wilma A. Medley and first appears in the 1959 city directory.

MEFFERT ROAD

Indian Neck
See Hudson Court

MELROSE AVENUE

Indian Neck, off Indian Neck Avenue to a dead end
Map #73 1918 Branford Gardens, owned and developed by John J. Linsky, 68 lots

The street was accepted as a town road in 1935[259] from John J. Linsky but does not appear until 1953 on the Price & Lee map. It was part of the Branford Gardens development.

MIDWOOD ROAD

Short Beach, off Shore Drive to a dead end
Map #805 1952 property of Arnold T. Peterson, owner and developer

The street was accepted as a town road in 1949[260] from Arnold J. and Alice T. Peterson. The street was developed and named for "middle of the woods" in 1949 by Arnold T. and Evangeline Peterson. It first appears on the 1953 Price & Lee map and an extension of the road was accepted in 1959[261] and again in 1971.

MILL CREEK PLACE

Off Mill Creek Road to a dead end

The street was accepted as a town road in 1941[262] and first appears on the 1953 Price & Lee map. It was part of the Ten Acres subdivision by builder Harold M. Roth and real estate agent William T. Beazley Company.

MILL CREEK ROAD

Off Driscoll Road and loops back to Driscoll
Map #263 1940 Ten Acres subdivision, property of Harold M. Roth

The street was accepted as a town road in 1941[263] and first appears in the 1942 city directory. The creek is referred to in 1648 "land at the neck where Tho: Mulliner somtyes dwelt & the river comonlie called the mill river."[264] The Mill Creek was also known as Oyster Neck Creek or Linsleys Creek.

MILL PLAIN ROAD

Mill Plain, off East Main Street, becomes Northford Road, Queach Road and Twin Lakes Road in North Branford

The Mill Plain section of Branford was settled in the 17th century and the street was a main route between Branford and North Branford. A mill is referred to in the Town Records as early as 1648 and the mill quarter and the mill by the great river [Branford River] is mentioned in 1681.[265] The 1868 Beers map refers to the area as the Mill Plain District. A small section of Mill Plain Road was called Maple Hill Road or Maple Hill Queach Road and appears with that name in the city directories or on the Price & Lee maps from 1926 until 1956. The house at 164 Mill Plain Road known as Maple Hill was built Lauren Palmer before 1850. Queach is a section in the western part of the Mill Plain District.

MILLER'S COURT

Short Beach
See Pentecost Street

Entrance of Mill Plain Road from East Main Street.

MILLWOOD DEVELOPMENT

Brushy Plain

This 150-acre property belonged to the Stent family since the 1600s and was developed in 1960[266] with two hundred homes by Edward Waltman of the Garry Builders Corporation of West Hartford. Four styles of homes were offered ranging in price from $15,999 to $17,990. See Ash Road, Cypress Drive, Hazel Drive, Hemlock Road, Locust Street, and Millwood Drive.

MILLWOOD DRIVE

Brushy Plain, off Brushy Plain Road to Cypress Drive, sometimes Millwood Road
Map #782 1959 owner and developer Branford Development Corporation as part of the Millwood subdivision

The street was accepted as a town road in 1961[267] from Edward Waltman Associates, Inc. and first appears on the 1964 Price & Lee map. The street was developed in phases.

MILO DRIVE

Damascus, off Damascus Road to a dead end, sometimes Windmill Hill Road Extension
Maps #635 & #793 1956 Louis W. Desi, owner & developer

The street was accepted as a town road in 1958[268] from Louis Desi and first appears in the 1960 city directory. The road was extended in 1964.[269] The street name is from the first two initials of Michael and Louis Desiderio (Desi).

MONA AVENUE

Branford Hills, off West Main Street to a dead end
Map #109 1924 Branford Heights, property of Thomas F. Reilly

The street was part of the Branford Heights development and was accepted as a town road in 1935[270] from Daniel W. Owens. It first appears on the 1936 Price & Lee map.

The Streets, Alphabetical 127

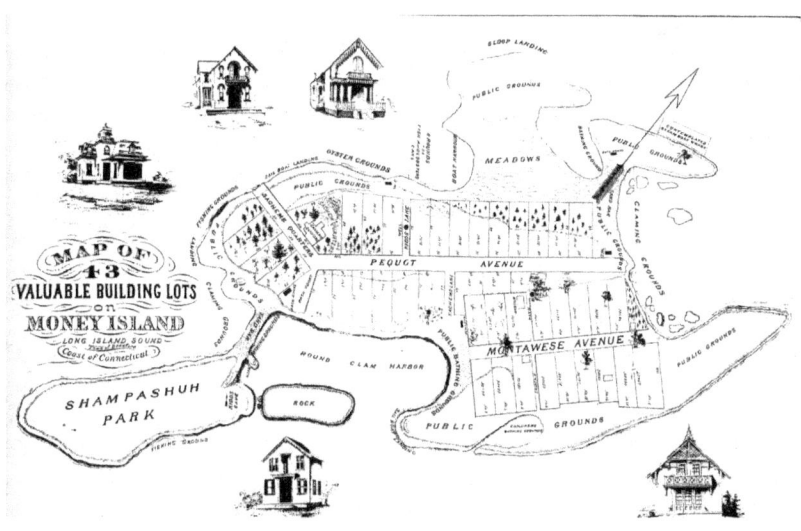

Map showing lots developed by Chauncey Dickerman on Money Island.

Cottages on Money Island in the early 1900s.

MONEY ISLAND

Stony Creek
Old Map #11- no date, 43 valuable building plots, Money Island

Several streets were named on the island when it was developed with building lots by Chauncey A. Dickerman in 1869. See Montowese Avenue, Sachems Lane, Sachems Quarter, and Pequot Avenue. One of the streets was sometimes called Kidds Lane. The streets and island are in the National Register Stony Creek Historic District.

MONROE PLACE

Branford Point
See Ely Street

MONROE STREET

Branford Center, off Main Street to Cherry Street

The street was put through about 1855 when Daniel T. Monroe[271] began selling lots and the street appears on the 1868 Beers map. The street was extended north in 1880.[272] The Monroe family came to Branford in the early 1700s. The street is in the National Register Branford Center Historic District.

MONTGOMERY PARKWAY

Pawson Park, off Linden Avenue to a dead end, sometimes Montgomery Road or Manor
Maps #366 & #383 Montgomery Parkway, proposed road off Linden Avenue and building lots, leaseholder Branford Realty Co.

The street appears on the 1924 Sanborn map and is named for General Phelps Montgomery, a summer resident at 113 Linden Avenue. Cottages were here in the early 1900s. The street was a private road owned by the First Ecclesiastical Society and was accepted as a town road in 1968.[273] Branford Realty Company was owned by Reginald S. Baldwin who was the leaseholder for many cottages in Pawson Park and in turn rented or leased them out.

The Streets, Alphabetical

MONTICELLO DRIVE
Branford Hills, off Jefferson Road looping back
Map #250c 1978 Jefferson Woods section three, Associated Builders Corp.

The street first appears in the 1973 city directory. The street is named for the home of Thomas Jefferson.

MONTOWESE AVENUE
Stony Creek

It is one of four streets on Money Island developed by Chauncey A. Dickerman in 1869.

MONTOWESE STREET
Branford Center, off Main Street south becoming South Montowese Street

The street was one of Branford's first two roads, both of which were called Towne Street, leading from the current Main Street to the Branford River. The street is named for Montowese, sachem of the

The John Foote House at 130 Montowese Street. Photo by Mason Foote Smith

Montowese Street in 1964. Photo by Earl Colter

Montowese Street at Main Street.

Quinnipiac Indians. The street was extended south across the river when Samuel Russell built a bridge in 1791 called the Lower Bridge, later called Hobart's Bridge (sometimes incorrectly spelled Hubbard). Montowese Street south to Indian Neck was a state road by 1917[274] and Connecticut State Highway- Route 146 in 1955. Montowese Street from South Main Street south became part of the National Register Route 146 scenic highway in 1996. The street is in the National Register Branford Center Historic District.

MONTOYA CIRCLE AND DRIVE

Cherry Hill, off Commercial Parkway to Cherry Hill Road

Montoya Circle was originally Cherry Hill Circle which first appears on the 1954 zoning map leading to the Cherry Hill apartments, part of the 300-acre Cherry Hill Estates development by the Sachs family. The name was changed about 1986 and the street expanded with the addition of Montoya Drive.

MONTVALE

Branford Hills
See Brainard Road, Claredon Street, Hoadley Road, Kenyon Street, and Matthew Road

MOUNTAIN TOP DRIVE

Brushy Plain, off Victor Hill Drive to a dead end
Map #1965 Mountain Top Estates subdivision, owner & developer J. M. Defelice Construction Co., Inc.

The street first appears in the 1968 city directory.

NEW PALMER ROAD

Branford Center
See Palmer Woods Circle

NEWTON ROAD

Indian Neck, off South Montowese Street to a dead end

The street first appears on the 1954 zoning map as Palmer Place or Road (see Isabel Lane). The street name was changed in 1958[275] because there was already a Palmer Road in Branford Center. The property belonged to James Palmer and it was renamed for the Walter Newton family.

NINTH AVENUE

See Hotchkiss Grove

NORTH BRANFORD

Branford originally included land north to Wallingford including present day North Branford and the village of Northford. North Branford was called the Second Society, North Parish or North Farms and was settled in the late 17th century. The first road to North Farms was through Hopyard Plain and is now North Branford Road. The road to Bare Plain, now Bushy Plain Road, was built in 1712 and becomes Totoket Road in North Branford. Northford was originally known as Paug, Salem, Goshen or the Third Society and was settled about 1725. North Branford remained under the jurisdiction of Branford until 1831 when the General Assembly voted to allow North Branford to become a separate town.

NORTH BRANFORD ROAD

Off East Main Street becomes Branford Road in North Branford

The street is a colonial road built in 1698 as the first road to North Branford, known as North Farms or the Second Society. It was once called Old Branford Road and today is designated as Route 139. The street is called Branford Road over the North Branford boundary line.

NORTH CHESTNUT STREET

Branford Center
See Chestnut Street

NORTH HARBOR STREET

Branford Center, off Main Street south, crossing Bradley Street
to Elm Street

This street is a colonial road and was probably here by 1700. Harbor Street coming from Branford Point originally went to Main Street but was bisected when the railroad came through in 1852. This section north of the railroad tracks has alternately been called Harbor or North Harbor Street. To add to the confusion, the town uses the post-1968 numbering system but some residents still use the old numbering system for their mailing address.

In the city directories from 1895 until 1958 it is called Harbor Street. On the 1914 and 1924 Sanborn maps it is listed as North Harbor Street. This northern stretch of Harbor Street is not labeled on the Price & Lee maps. From 1928 until 1958 the houses have a Harbor Street address with high house numbers (i.e. 464 Harbor Street). In 1958, it was proposed that the section of Bradley Street between West Main Street and Bridge Street be renamed Kelly Street.[276] This proposal was rejected. The street name was changed in 1958 to North Harbor Street but the houses numbers stayed the same. (i.e. 464 North Harbor Street) About 1968 the house numbers changed to low numbers (464 North Harbor Street became 23 North Harbor Street).[277]

NORTH IVY STREET

See Ivy Street

NORTH MAIN STREET

Branford Center, from West Main Street to East Main Street, also known as the Cut Off, Route 1 or 1A

A proposal to build a new road to bypass the center of town was first discussed in 1930. There was opposition from business owners in Branford Center. The road was built in 1932 under the Federal Aid Emergency Projects.[278] The contractor was D. V. Frione Company of New Haven and subcontractor John T. Sliney of Branford. The street opened on July 8, 1933 as a state road.[279] The new Cut Off was named North Main Street and accepted as a town road in 1935.[280] The street first appears with a Route 1 label in 1963.

NORTHAM STREET

Stony Creek
See Leetes Island Road

North Main Street looking east at Cedar Street. Photo by Earl Colter

The Streets, Alphabetical | 135

NORTHFORD ROAD

Mill Plain, Mill Plain Road becomes Northford Road, the end of Northford Road sometimes called Queach Road; see Queach Road
Map #923 1965 a portion of the road was part of the development by Brookhills, Inc.

Northford Road is a colonial road connecting Mill Plain to North Branford. It appears as Queach Road on the early Price & Lee maps, making two Queach Roads- one branching off Mill Plain Road to the northwest and this one to the northeast. The name Northford Road first appears in the 1942 city directory for the section leading to North Branford.

OAK STREET

Off West End Avenue to a dead end
See Evergreen Place

The street first appears on the 1959 Price & Lee map on property belonging to the Malleable Iron Fittings Company.

OAK STREET

Short Beach
See Glen Street

OAKDALE PLACE

Blackstone Acres, off Riverside Drive to Woodvale Road, see also Oakdale Road
Map #695 1956 section two of the Blackstone Acres development

The street was accepted as a town road in 1959[281] from Sturgess & Jockmus, Inc. and first appears in the 1960 city directory.

OAKDALE ROAD

Blackstone Acres, off Riverside Drive to Oakdale Place, see also Oakdale Place
Map #590 1956 section two of the Blackstone Acres development

The street was accepted as a town road in 1958[282] from Buza, Sturgess & Jockmus Company and first appears in the city directory the same year.

OAKGATE DRIVE

Off Featherbed Lane to Wellsweep Road
Map #753 1961 Oakgate development by Anderson-Wilcox, Co.

The street first appears in the 1964 city directory and was accepted as a town road in 1965[283] from Anderson-Wilcox Company.

OAK HOLLOW ROAD

Off Pine Orchard Road to a dead end
Map #1025 1968 owned and developed by Christopher Reynolds and Joseph Meshako

The street first appears in the 1970 city directory and was accepted as a town road in 1971.[284]

OAK RIDGE ROAD

Indian Neck, off Frank Street to Hickory Road
Map #459 1945 building lots on Oak Ridge Road, property of the MIF

The street was accepted as a town road in 1958[285] from the Malleable Iron Fittings Company and first appears on the 1959 Price & Lee map.

O'BRIEN ROAD

Brushy Plain, off Todds Hill Road looping back to Todds Hill
Map #634 1955 Todds Hill Heights, O'Brien Road

The street was accepted as a town road in 1948[286] from Daniel Cosgrove and first appears in the 1950 city directory. Daniel O'Brien was born in Ireland and came to Branford in 1854, settling at Todds Hill. His daughter Elizabeth O'Brien married James Cosgrove.

OLD BRANFORD ROAD

See North Branford Road

OLD FARM HOUSE ROAD

Pine Orchard
See Sunset Hill Road

OLD HICKORY LANE

Mill Plain, off Ridge Acres Road and loops back
Map #515 1953 part of Ridge Acres development, property of Frederic Rosenthal

Old Hickory Lane was accepted as a town road in 1954[287] and extensions in 1957, 1958, and 1961 from Frederic Rosenthal. The street first appears on the 1956 Price & Lee map.

OLD NEW ENGLAND ROAD

Stony Creek, off Flat Rock Road to Quarry Road
Map #1343 1967, received 1978, New Quarry Road

The street first appears on the 1980 Exchange Club map.

OLD PAWSON LANDING

Indian Neck
See Pawson Landing Road

OLD PAWSON ROAD

Indian Neck, off Linden Avenue to Pawson Road, sometimes Old Pawson Park Road, Sioux Place
See Hudson Court
Map #34 1910 proposed road
Maps #709 & #823 1950, received 1958 First Ecclesiastical Society

The street was built in the early 1900s. The street had a slightly different configuration, was more curved and had two small branches with a triangle as it came off Linden Avenue. The street appears on the 1924 map but the portion off Linden Avenue is called Hudson Court, the road made a sharp left turn onto Old Pawson Road then west to Pawson Road. It has the same designation on the 1994 Exchange Club map; however, the entire stretch is called Old Pawson Road on the 1954 Zoning map. The street was a private road owned by the First Ecclesiastical Society and the street was accepted as a town road in 1968.[288]

OLD PINE ORCHARD ROAD

Branford Center, off Montowese Street to a dead end
See also Pine Orchard Road, sometimes Robinson's Road
Map #1109 1969 part of Pine Orchard Road now abandoned

The 1868 Beers map has a road from 15 Pine Orchard Road (The Blackstone House) across the Branford River to Little Plain. This road was abandoned.

Old Pine Orchard Road was built in 1882[289] replacing the above route to Damascus. The wooden bridge across the river was rebuilt in 1914.[290] A new bridge was built in 1962 with a reconfigured entrance at Montowese Street and Pine Orchard Road.[291] The Old Pine Orchard Bridge or Blackstone Bridge was torn down the same year[292] and Old Pine Orchard Road now ends at the river.

OLD POST ROAD

See Boston Post Road

OLD SHORT BEACH ROAD

Branford Hills
See Alps Road

The Old Pine Orchard Road bridge was removed in 1962. Photo by Earl Colter.

OLD SMUGGLERS ROAD

Branford Point, off Stannard Avenue and loops back
Map #662 1956 section B of Jourdan Farm, Fannie Jourdan et al

The street was accepted as a town road in 1957[293] from Fannie E. Jourdan et al and first appears on the 1960 Price & Lee map. It is named for the smuggling trade- goods were taken off boats at Branford Point and brought inland. This oral tradition predates the Depression. James Bradley of Short Beach asked old timers if there was any truth that the road was used in the 1800s for smuggling. They said there was no proof, but the road was used by ships to transport goods inland from the Branford Point dock.[294]

OLD STONY CREEK ROAD

See Damascus Road

OLD TOWN ROAD

See Pine Orchard Road

ORCHARD AVENUE

Hotchkiss Grove, off Hotchkiss Grove Road to a dead end, sometimes Orchard Road or Home Place

The street is on the north side of Hotchkiss Grove and appears on the 1924 Sanborn map. Homer Griffing had a house here and developed the street in 1957. It is part of the Hotchkiss Grove Association.

ORCHARD HILL ROAD

Branford Hills, off West Main Street to Florence Road
Maps #484, 500, 550 & 514 1952 property of Sarah Harrison Jones to Peter Powers Hale

The street was accepted as a town road in 1954[295] from Sarah Harrison Jones whose family owned 1021 West Main Street at the corner of Alps Road. An extension was accepted by the town in 1956[296] from Builder's Group, Inc. It is named for the apple and peach orchards that once stood on Branford Hills. In 2015 a few of the old trees were still along the street. The development, built by the Builders Group, was the first housing project in the New Haven area to win the Certified Quality Design seal of the Housing Research Foundation. The houses were designed by Peter Powers Hale of New Haven.[297]

ORCHARD LANE

See Goldsmith Road

OVERLAND COURT

Brushy Plain, off Brushy Plain Road to a dead end, sometimes Overland Drive
Map #917 1965 Laurel Acres development by Gargano Construction Co.

The street was accepted as a town road in 1967[298] and first appears in the city directory the same year.

OWENS PLACE

Short Beach
See Jefferson Place

OZONE ROAD

Pine Orchard, off Selden Avenue to Pasadena Road, sometimes Ozone Avenue
Map #23 1907 Blackstone Park owned by F. C. Bradley

The street was part of the Blackstone Park development. The lots were sold in 1907 by real estate agent Frederick Curtis Bradley who wintered in Pasadena, California. The street was named by him. Bradley was known as the Mayor of Pine Orchard.[299]

PALMER AVENUE

Indian Neck
See Limewood Avenue

PALMER HEIGHTS

Indian Neck
See Isabel Lane

PALMER PLACE OR ROAD

Indian Neck
See Newton Road

PALMER ROAD

Branford Center, off Cedar Street to Palmer Woods Circle
Maps #116 & #151 1925 & 1929 property of Harriet L. Palmer

The street first appears in the 1926 city directory and was accepted as a town road in 1932[300] from Harriet L. Palmer of 740 Main Street.

PALMER ROAD

Stony Creek
See Thimble Islands Road

PALMER WOODS CIRCLE

Branford Center, off Palmer Road, sometimes New Palmer Road or Palmer Woods Terrace
Map #481 & #497 1951 property of Ray U. Plant showing building lots
Map #553 1955 Palmer Woods Circle, Totoket Construction Co.

The street first appears in the 1953 city directory and was accepted as a town road in 1955[301] from Ray U. Plant. Plant received the Palmer family holdings after the death of his business partner Walter Palmer in 1949.

PARISH FARM ROAD

Brushy Plain, off Brushy Plain Road to Todds Hill Road

The street appears on the 1852 Whiteford map connecting Brushy Plain with Todds Hill. There are no buildings marked on the 1868 Beers map. It was probably named for the Parish family who came to Branford in the early 18th century. Most of the street was developed with houses in the 1950s.

PARK PLACE

Branford Center, off Main Street to Rose Street, sometimes Park Avenue

The street appears by 1895 and was also called Lay-Toole or LaToole Avenue. A portion was accepted as a town road in 1922[302] and another portion in 1932[303] from Thomas J. Toole. Where the entrance from Main Street is today was once the home of Dr. Willoughby Lay. The street is in the National Register Branford Center Historic District.

PARK PLACE

Pine Orchard
See Chapel Drive and Lake Avenue

PARKER MEMORIAL PARK DRIVE

Branford Point, off Harbor Street, sometimes Parker Memorial Drive

The road leads to summer cottages built in the 1880s and 1890s. The street and cottages are privately owned and do not belong to the Town of Branford as part of Parker Park. It is named for Dr. Frank Parker who donated the park to the Town of Branford in 1914. The street is in the National Register Branford Point Historic District.

PARKER PLACE

Branford Point, off Harbor Street to a dead end

The street first appears on the 1924 Sanborn map but was probably here earlier. It is named for George and Alice (Lanphier) Parker who owned 65 Harbor Street and other property. In 1947 Parker Place was a private road. The street is in the National Register Branford Point Historic District.

PARTING PATHS

See Damascus Road

PASADENA ROAD

Pine Orchard, off Selden Avenue to Spring Rock Road
Map #23 1907 Blackstone Park owned by F. C. Bradley

The street was part of the Blackstone Park development. Lots were sold in 1907 by real estate agent Frederick C. Bradley whose original cottage was at the corner of Pasadena Road and Selden Avenue. His family wintered in Pasadena, California and the street was named by him.

The Streets, Alphabetical 143

PATRICK LANE

Damascus, off Damascus Road to a dead end
Map #758 1960 owner and developer Fred Corbin

The street first appears in the 1964 city directory and was accepted as a town road in 1966.[304] It was part of twenty-five acres sold to Robert Patrick in 1929.[305]

PAVED STREET

Stony Creek
See Leetes Island Road; sometimes Old Paved Street, Flat Rock Road, Old Highway

Paved Street was a term for part of Leetes Island Road generally from East Main Street south to the junction of Stony Creek, Leetes Island, and Thimble Islands Roads. The street was built and named by 1767[306] when several houses were built. It is presumed that part of the road was "paved" perhaps with cobblestones. The Paved

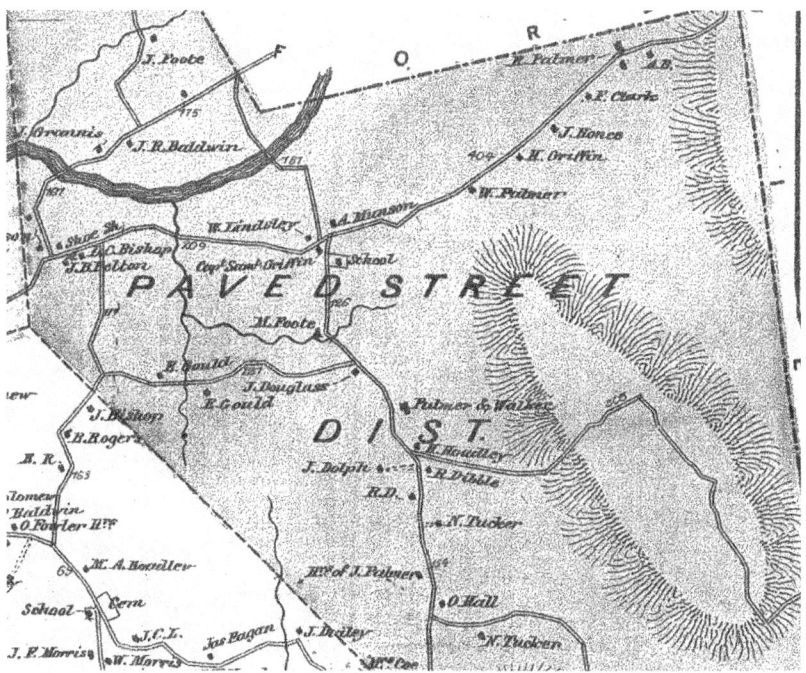

The Paved Street District from the 1868 Beers New Haven County Atlas.

Street District appears on the 1868 Beers map and included west to Featherbed Lane (then Totoket Road), north to the North Branford line, east to the Guilford line and south just beyond Flat Rock Road. A portion along Paved Street was also sometimes called Flat Rock Road. There was a Paved Street School until 1929. Older residents still call the northern part of Leetes Island Road by the old name.

The junction of East Main Street, Paved Street, and School Ground Road was called Pranns, Granniss, or Four Corners for the families that lived at 569 East Main Street. This corner was reconfigured in the late 20th century.

PAVILION COURT

Short Beach, off Court Street to a dead end, sometimes Pavilion Drive or Grove
Map #932 1966 Pavilion Grove, 5 lots, owner Michael Dombrowski

The street was accepted as a town road in 1966[307] and first appears in the 1968 city directory. It is named for the dance pavilion that once stood here.

Pawson Park was a summer resort with a skating rink that is now a home on Wakefield Road. Photo by Frank W. Jerold.

PAWSON LANDING ROAD

Indian Neck, off Old Pawson Road to a dead end, sometimes Pawson Landing Drive or Old Pawson Landing
Map #987 1968 owner and developer Anderson-Wilcox, Inc.

The street was accepted as a town road in 1969[308] and first appears in the 1971 city directory. Anderson-Wilcox purchased the land from Robert Meffert.

PAWSON PARK

Indian Neck

The First Ecclesiastical Society of Branford owned much of the land from Linden Avenue west purchasing it directly from the Totoket Indians in the early 18th century. The Society leased the land in 1866 for ninety-nine years and people built cottages, owning the buildings but not the land. The area was farmed and in 1884 the Pawson Park Amusement Park was built by the Samuel Beach family including an ice skating rink, carousel, restaurant, photograph gallery, and cottages. Pawson was a sachem of the Totoket Indians. The amusement park lasted until 1903 but the area continued as a summer cottage community. By the mid-20th century the lease came due and the Ecclesiastical Society decided to sell the land, offering it to the current lease holders. The Society had their entire holdings surveyed in 1958 by engineer Charles H. Miller in a series of four maps. Shortly afterwards some of the street names were changed by the town.

In 1960 a request was made to the Board of Selectmen to accept all the Society's private roads as town roads. The Town of Branford had already been plowing and repairing the roads for many years. The Board of Selectmen denied the request- the roads were too narrow and had inadequate drainage.[309] The request was again brought before the Representative Town Meeting (RTM) in 1968[310] to accept all the Ecclesiastical Society's private roads from the 1958 maps. The RTM recommended the streets be accepted in fairness to the Pawson Park residents and the recommendation was passed by the Board of Selectmen.[311]

PAWSON ROAD

Indian Neck, off Linden Avenue to a dead end at the Branford River, sometimes Sowheag Path or Pawson Park Road
Map #709 1950, received 1958 First Ecclesiastical Society, refers to Sowheag Path

Pawson Road was the main road to the Pawson Park summer resort which was built in 1884. The portion of Pawson Park Road from Wakefield Road north to the peninsula was called Sowheag Path. That road appears on maps as either Sowheag Path or Pawson Park Road. Today's designation of Pawson Road, being the entire road from Linden Avenue to River Road first appears in the 1950 city directory. The street was a private road owned by the First Ecclesiastical Society and was accepted as a town road in 1968.[312]

PAWSON TRAIL ROAD

Indian Neck, off River Road, crossing Pawson Road to a dead end
Map #499 1952 estate of V. T. Hammer

The street was built in the late 19th century when Pawson Park was a summer resort. The street was a private road owned by the First Ecclesiastical Society and was accepted as a town road in 1968.[313] Valdemar T. Hammer, among others, had a summer cottage here.

PAYNES POINT ROAD

Short Beach, off Clark Avenue to a dead end

It is a private road off Clark Avenue named for Thomas Payne who owned a cottage here by the 1870s. The street name appears on some maps and is used as a mailing address by the residents. The town uses a Clark Avenue address for their records.

PEDDLERS DRIVE

Branford Hills
See The Greens

The Streets, Alphabetical

PENT ROAD

Branford Hills, off West Main Street to Rose Hill Road

A pent road in New England refers to a road that is enclosed by gates or bars especially at its terminal point. The street first appears in the 1925 city directory and was probably the new highway built by the town in 1913[314] south of Route 1 leading to farms on the southern side of Branford Hills.

PENTECOST STREET

Short Beach, off Shore Drive to a dead end
Map #210 1933 showing original layout of Pentecost Street

The street was put through and lots sold in 1880 by Ezra and Hiram Clark (father and son) who had large land holdings in Short Beach. The Short Beach Union Church was built in 1883 and the street is named for Pentecost which marks the seventh Sunday after Easter. The street was accepted as a town road in 1933.[315] A private driveway east off Pentecost Street led to houses called Miller's Court, also known as Clam Alley or Lobster Row. This driveway is also referred to in a deed as Clark Avenue.

Pentecost Street looking south to the water. The Short Beach Union Church, built in 1883, is on the right. Photo postcard by the Garraway Company.

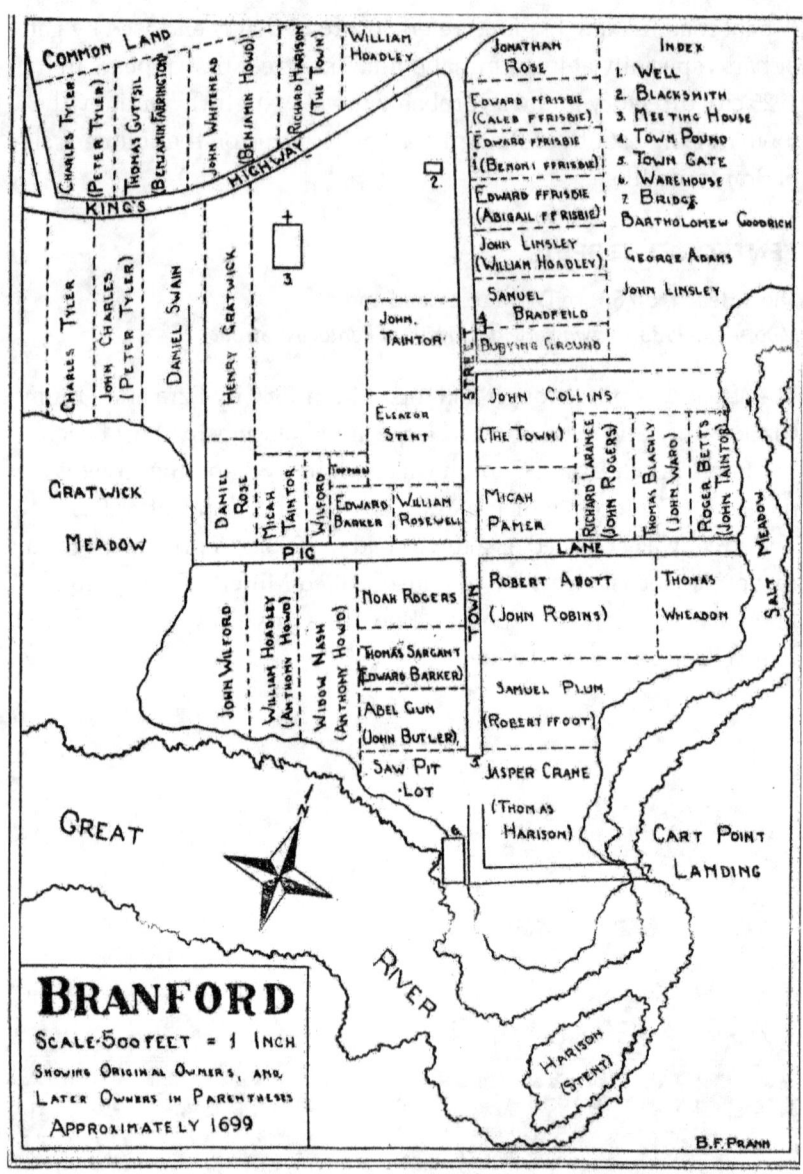

A map by Bradley F. Prann from Old Branford *by John C. Carr depicts the roads and home lots in 1699.*

PEQUOT AVENUE

Stony Creek

It is one of three streets on Money Island developed by Chauncey A. Dickerman in 1869.

PETER BRIDGE ROAD

Sometimes Peters Bridge Road, see Ark Road

The highway to Peters Bridge appears as early as 1682.[316]

PIG LANE

Branford Center

Pig Lane was an original street built by the first settlers crossing about where 116 Montowese Street is today. It ran from Hammer Field to the Branford River behind Center Cemetery. The road has long been abandoned.

PINE HOLLOW ROAD

Brushy Plain, off Red Rock Road to Bear Path Road
Map #1239 1975 Laurel Hill subdivision, owner and developer Herbert Small

The street first appears in the 1977 city directory and was accepted as a town road in 1978.[317]

PINE ORCHARD

Also called World's End, Brown Point, Great Plain, Long Marsh
Maps #816 and #342 Pine Orchard zoning

Pine Orchard is a section of Branford along the shore between Hotchkiss Grove and Stony Creek. The area was called World's End, named for the creek east of today's Pine Orchard Club and the name first appears in 1668.[318] The Sheldon, Baldwin, and Pierpont families lived here by the early 19th century and the area was developed later as a summer resort and cottage community. The name Pine Orchard appears in 1842.[319]

Pine Orchard was originally called World's End for the creek that runs east of today's Pine Orchard Club.

A new bridge connecting Branford Center and Damascus was built in 1962 behind the Branford Armory. Photo by Earl Colter.

PINE ORCHARD ROAD

Off Montowese Street to Elizabeth Street then east to Totoket Road
Old Map #8 1896 proposed new road at Ben Barker's hill
See also Totoket Road, Damascus Road, locally called Cathedral Isle[320]

The street appears on the 1852 Whiteford map leading from Damascus Road to about where Elizabeth Street is today. The designation of Pine Orchard Road has changed over time. The portion from Montowese Street to Damascus was also known as Blackstone's Road. A small portion of the road now 157 Pine Orchard Road was once known as Old Town Road.[321]

Damascus Road was accessed via Old Pine Orchard Road at the end of Montowese Street, over a wooden bridge, exiting in front of 18 Pine Orchard Road. The section of road from Island View Avenue to about where the Pine Orchard Club is today was built in 1897.[322] The portion just east of the Pine Orchard Club was called Sheldon Road and turning north becoming Pine Orchard Road again north to Damascus Cemetery.

Between 1939 and 1946 Pine Orchard Road continued east past the Pine Orchard Club and included the former Sheldon Road. The portion going north became Totoket Road. The route of Pine Orchard Road was formerly set in 1958[323] as being from Montowese Street to Totoket Road which is the street designation today. A short stretch of Pine Orchard Road from Elizabeth Street to Blackstone Avenue became part of the Connecticut State Highway System- Route 146 in 1962[324] and as part of the National Register Route 146 scenic highway in 1996.

PINE TREE DRIVE

Off Stony Creek Road to a dead end
Map #951 1966 part of The Pines subdivision, owner and developer Sturgess & Co.

The street was accepted as a town road in 1969[325] and first appears in the 1970 city directory.

PINEWOOD ROAD

Pine Orchard, off Meadow Wood Road to a dead end
Map #844 1963 Pinewood development, property of Josephine Giordano

The street first appears on the 1965 Price & Lee map and was accepted as a town road in 1966.[326]

PINSKI DRIVE

Branford Hills, off Rose Hill Road to a dead end, sometimes Pinski Road
Maps #487, #521 & #582 1951 & 1953 owner and developer Benjamin D. Pinski

The street was accepted as a town road in 1950[327] from Benjamin D. Pinski and was part of the Saltonstall Park development. The street first appears in the 1953 city directory.

PISCITELLO DRIVE

Brushy Plain, off Laurel Hill Road to a dead end
Map #637 1956 land of John and Anna Piscitello, owners and developers

The street was accepted as a town road in 1954[328] from John and Anna Piscitello and first appears in the 1956 city directory. The street was extended by the same owners in 1961. The Piscitello family came to Branford about 1908.

PLANT ROAD

Off Short Beach Road to a dead end
Map #530 1951 building lots on land of Albert B. Plant off Short Beach Road
Map #533 1954 Northern Maple Corners, property of Ray U. Plant

The street was accepted as a town road in 1956[329] from Ray U. Plant and first appears on the 1959 Price & Lee map. John Plant came to Branford in 1677.

PLANT'S ROCK PASTURE ROAD

See Rock Pasture Road

The Streets, Alphabetical | 153

PLANTSVILLE

Branford Hills
See Branford Hills

PLEASANT POINT ROAD

Off Totoket Road to a dead end, formerly Bush's Neck, Vedder's Point, Vedder Road, Point Pleasant, Bush Neck Road, Farm Road, a portion was called Meadow Road

The peninsula became known as Bush's Neck when Gilbert Bush purchased land and a dwelling from Simeon Frisbie in 1811.[330] Grace Bush married Francis Vedder of New York in 1838 and the Vedder family owned property here until 2007. The Vedder family called it Point Pleasant.

PLYMOUTH COLONY

Off Alps Road and loops back
Map #123c 1972 Westcor Development Corporation

The condominium complex has a Plymouth Colony address.

POINT ROAD

Branford Point
See Harbor Street

POMPANO AVENUE

Branford Hills, off West Main Street to Donna Lane, sometimes Pompano Drive or Lane
Map #370 1948 lot layout for Patsy Pompano

The street was accepted as a town road in 1949[331] and an extension in 1966 from Josephine (Leonardo) Pompano. The street first appears on the 1950 Price & Lee map. The Pompano family came to Branford about 1915.

POOR HOUSE ROAD

Damascus
See Damascus Road

PROPRIETOR'S ROAD

Branford Hills
See Alex-Warfield Road

PROSPECT HILL ROAD

Stony Creek, off Thimble Islands Road east to a dead end, formerly Camp's or Camp Hill, sometimes Prospect Avenue, Point or Street, Fairview Avenue
Map #539 Prospect Street in Stony Creek 1880, Henry Rogers to Cyrus Hart
Map #329 1936 Prospect Hill Road Extension, change in layout

The street was developed and lots sold by Cyrus Hart who purchased the land from Henry Rogers in 1871.[332] Map #539 calls it Fairview Avenue. It was known as Camp's Hill named for cottage owner Theron Camp. Rosalind Pratt of "Villa Vista" at 32 Prospect Hill is listed in the 1907 city directory as living at Camp Hill Flying Point and in 1913 as Prospect Hill Flying Point. The street is in the National Register Stony Creek Historic District. North from the end of Prospect Hill is the former Big and Little Brooklyn Quarries.

Prospect Hill in Stony Creek was formerly called Camp's Hill. Photo postcard by Edward W. Quimby.

The Streets, Alphabetical | 155

PROSPECT STREET

Branford Center, from Hopson Avenue east to Church Street
Old Map, no number, 1916 Extension of Prospect Street to Church Street

The street was built by the town in 1903[333] and first appears on the 1905 Bird's-Eye map from Hopson Avenue to Eades Street. It was extended through to Church Street in 1916 and the entire street appears on the 1924 Sanborn map. The street was accepted as a town road in 1932[334] from the street's owners. The street is in the National Register Branford Center Historic District.

PROSPECT STREET

Stony Creek
See Prospect Hill Road and Ridge Road

PUBLIC DOCK ROAD

Stony Creek
See Indian Point Road

QUARRY ROAD

Stony Creek, off Leetes Island Road to a dead end, sometimes Stony Creek Quarry Road, see also Seastrand Road

The street first appears in the 1953 city directory as Quarry Road and as Stony Creek Quarry Road on the 1954 zoning map. The road leads to a granite quarry still in use today. Old Quarry Road, associated with the former Beattie Quarry, is just over the border in Guilford. Quarry Dock Road in Indian Neck is part of the Sylvan Point condominium complex built in the 1980s.

QUARRY ROAD

Stony Creek
See School Street

QUEACH

Queach is a section in the northern part of town between Brushy Plain and Hopyard Plain and includes Short Rocks. There is also a Queach Brook. The name first appears in the town records in 1679 "head of ye Swamp that runs from ye head of Cannow Brook to ye queach.[335] In old English queach was a thick, bushy plot or thicket.

QUEACH ROAD

Mill Plain, off Mill Plain Road to a dead end
Map #458 1950 lots sold by Frederic Rosenthal
Map #1087 1969 section five by Brookhills, Inc.

The street appears on the 1852 Whiteford map off Mill Plain Road. It connected to what today is Laurel Hill Road where the Edgar Page family had a farm. The area of the Page farm was known as Knockers Hole. Queach Road connecting to Laurel Hill still appears on the Price & Lee and Exchange Club maps through the 1990s. Today that portion is abandoned. Northford Road was also called Queach Road making two Queach Roads, one branching off Mill Plain Road to the northwest and one to the north. The northern Queach Road's name was changed to Northford Road which first appears in the 1942 city directory. Though a colonial road, much of Queach Road was not developed until the mid to late twentieth century.

Northford Road was found on maps until 2014 for the entire northern section. Recently, various maps designate a portion of Northford Road north of #275 as Queach Road and a portion over the boundary of North Branford also as Queach Road, then becoming Twin Lakes Road. The Town of Branford uses Northford Road for the street addresses for the entire stretch of road to North Branford.

RAILROAD AVENUE

Branford Center
See Meadow Street

RAILROAD AVENUE

Stony Creek
See Bowhay Hill Road

RAMBLEWOOD DRIVE

Mill Plain, off Mill Plain Road and becomes Buttermilk Lane
Map #791 1962 part of the Ramblewood development by G & S Corporation

The street was accepted as a town road in 1964[336] from the Anderson-Wilcox Company and first appears in the city directory the same year. The original name was Susan Drive on the subdivision map.

RED HILL ROAD

Stony Creek, off Leetes Island Road to a dead end

The street appears on the 1852 map leading to what became the Red Hill and Norcross Quarries. Property at "Red Hill" appears in town records in 1805.[337] The street is named for Copperheads, also called red snake.[338]

RED ROCK ROAD

Brushy Plain, off Laurel Hill Road to a dead end
Map #1239 1975 Laurel Hill subdivision, owner and developer Herbert Small

The street first appears in the 1977 city directory and was accepted as a town road in 1978.[339]

REDWOOD ROAD

Damascus, off Windmill Hill Road to Victoria Drive
Map #691 1956 owners and developers John and Charles M. Maturo

The street was accepted as a town road in 1962[340] and first appears in the city directory the same year. The street was originally designated as Maturo Drive on the map.

REXTILE ROAD

Stony Creek, off Thimble Islands Road to Ridge Road

The street first appears in the 1926 city directory and may have been built in the early 1900s. The source of the name was not determined.

REYNOLDS AVENUE

Off Maple Street to Bryan Road
Map #421 & #469 1949 property of the Malleable Iron Fittings Company

The street was accepted as a town road in 1949[341] from the Malleable Iron Fittings Company and first appears in the 1956 city directory.

REYNOLDS LANE

Off Maple Street north to West End Avenue, sometimes Reynolds Street

The street first appears in the 1925 city directory and is named for the James T. Reynolds family. The Reynolds family came to Branford from Ireland about 1859.

RICE ROAD

Indian Neck, off Limewood Avenue north to a dead end, sometimes Rices Road

The street appears on the 1924 Sanborn map opposite West Haycock Point Road. The street is named for George and Elvira (Pond) Rice who ran the Limewood Grove House from 1880 until 1940. The site of the hotel is now the Breakers Condominiums. It still appears on maps but is not an official town road.

RICE TERRACE

Branford Center, off Montowese Street to a dead end
Map #858 1963 land of Leonial E. Rice, Jr.

The street first appears on the 1950 Price & Lee map. The Rice Terrace Senior Housing was built in 1978 by Annex Associates.[342] The street is in the National Register Branford Center Historic District.

RIDGE ACRES ROAD

Mill Plain, off Northford Road to a dead end
Map #515 1953 property of Frederic Rosenthal

The street was accepted as a town road in 1952 and extensions in 1955, 1961 and 1977[343] from Frederic Rosenthal. The street first appears in the 1953 city directory. Frederic Rosenthal purchased

The Streets, Alphabetical | 159

45 acres for 45 single family houses and the architect was Gordon Macmaster. A portion of the road was developed in 1965 by Brookhills, Inc.

RIDGE ROAD
Indian Neck
See Fenway Road

RIDGE ROAD
Stony Creek, off Thimble Islands Road to a dead end, originally called Prospect Road or Street

The street does not appear on the 1868 Beers and was built by 1892. It was called Ridge Road by 1917. The street is in the National Register Stony Creek Historic District.

RIDGE LANE
Blackstone Acres
See Woodvale Road

Thimble Islands Road (then Main Street) at Ridge Road in Stony Creek.

RIDGE ROCK ROAD
Brocketts Point
See Howard Avenue

RIVER ROAD
Pawson Park, off Pawson Road to a dead end, see Riverview Terrace

The street appears on the 1930 Price & Lee map without a name and the cottages were built about 1920. The street was a private road owned by the First Ecclesiastical Society and was accepted as a town road in 1968.[344]

RIVERSIDE DRIVE
Blackstone Acres, off Pine Orchard Road to a dead end
Map #663 & 695 1956 Blackstone Acres developed by Buza, Sturgess & Jockmus Co.

The street was accepted as a town road in 1958[345] from Buza, Sturgess & Jockmus Company and first appears the city directory the same year. An extension was accepted in 1960.[346]

RIVERSIDE TERRACE
Pawson Park
Map #705 1950 First Ecclesiastical Society

The street is along the water connecting River Road and Pawson Trail. It appears on some maps during the 1960s until 1994. The street was a private road owned by the First Ecclesiastical Society and was accepted as a town road in 1968.[347] By 1997 it was part of River Road.

RIVERVIEW AVENUE
Short Beach, off Highland Avenue and loops to Clark Avenue
Map #387 1946 Highland Park, property of Jennie B. Prout

Cottages were built on the street in the early 1900s. A street called Crest Avenue connecting Riverview Avenue and Highland Avenue appears on a 1914 map.[348]

ROBERT FROST DRIVE

Branford Hills
See *The Greens*

ROBINSON'S ROAD

See *Old Pine Orchard Road*

ROBY COURT

Branford Hills, off Alps Road to a dead end
Map #792 1962 part of the Briarwood development

The street first appears in the 1970 city directory and was accepted as a town road in 1971.[349]

ROCK PASTURE ROAD

Branford Point, off Stannard Avenue, sometimes Plant's Rock Pasture Road
Map #592 1956 land of Ray U. Plant

The street was accepted as a town road in 1956[350] from Ray U. Plant and first appears in the 1960 city directory. There was an earlier Rock Pasture Road which was widened and straightened in 1880.[351] This was perhaps the short road on the 1852 map connecting Short Beach Road to the Jourdan farm which is today the west end of Stannard Avenue.

ROCK STREET

Brushy Plain

It is an undeveloped road off Brushy Plain Road near the North Branford-Branford-East Haven border. The street appears on the 1930 Price & Lee map without a name and first appears as Rock Street in the 1960 Branford city directory. It is alternately called road or street. It is officially a street in East Haven and appears on the 1868 Beers map for that town.

ROCKLAND COURT

Blackstone Acres
See *Wildwood Drive*

ROCKLAND PARK ROAD

Short Beach, off Clark Avenue to a dead end, sometimes Rustic Road, Reynolds Avenue
Map #79 1915 estate of William Reynolds

Harrison Bristol of Cheshire had extensive land holdings in Short Beach. In 1872[352] he sold land to Dr. Sanford J. Horton of Cheshire and Henry Reynolds of New Haven. The road was developed with summer cottages and remains a private road. Some maps and deeds refer to Reynolds Avenue.

ROCKY LEDGE LANE

Blackstone Acres, off Wildwood Drive to a dead end, sometimes Rocky Road
Map #555 1955 Blackstone Acres section one

The street was accepted as a town road in 1956[353] and was originally named Glendale Court. The street name was changed in 1958[354] because there was already a Glendale Place in Short Beach. It was part of the Blackstone Acres development by Buza, Sturgess & Jockmus Company.

ROGERS ROAD

Stony Creek
See Sachem Road

ROGERS STREET

Branford Center, from Main Street to Meadow Street

Elizur Rogers sold lots in the 1850s and 1860s and the street appears on the 1856 map. It originally went through to the train depot in front of the Malleable Iron Fittings Company until Meadow Street was put through in 1894. The street is in the National Register Branford Center Historic District.

ROLLING HILL ROAD
Brushy Plain, off Laurel Hill Road to Red Rock Road
Map #1377 1977 Phase 2, Laurel Hill

The street was part of the Laurel Hill subdivision, owner and developer Herbert Small. It first appears in the 1978 city directory.

ROSE STREET
Branford Center, off Ivy Street to Cedar Street

The street first appears in the 1928 city directory and was put through about that time by Robert Rosenthal who owned the former Branford Lock Works buildings at Main and Ivy Streets. The road was named for Rose or Rose's Brook. The entrance was originally off Main Street between Veto and Ivy Streets to a dead end. The brook and wetlands were covered and drained in 1937[355] under the Works Project Administration (WPA). Rose Street was connected to Veto Street and Hillside Avenue in 1952 with the entrance still coming off Main Street. As part of the Center Revitalization in 1987, the entrance off Main Street was closed and a new access constructed off Ivy Street. As part of this project, Rose Street was continued connecting through to Cedar Street.

The entrance to Rockland Park from Clark Avenue.

ROSE HILL ROAD

Branford Hills, off West Main Street to a dead end
Map #42 1910 Saltonstall Park, land of William and Horace Chidsey
Map #717 1941, received 1958 Pleasant View Homes on Brooklawn Terrace and Rose Hill Road by Brooklawn Realty Co.

The street is named on the 1910 map and appears in the 1925 city directory. It was accepted as a town road in 1928.[356] Much of the street was developed later and the new section accepted as a town road in 1950[357] from Brooklawn Realty Company. It is perhaps named for the Rose family, first settlers of Branford.

ROUTE 1

Route 1 was designated in 1922 when the states throughout New England began a regional numbering system. Connecticut's portion of Route 1 was the coastal route generally following the Boston Post Road from Greenwich to the Rhode Island border. In 1926 the Federal government began a nationwide route numbering system and New England's Route 1 became part of U. S. Route 1 stretching from Maine to Florida.

In Branford, Route 1 started at the East Haven border, over West Main Street in the Branford Hills, along Main Street in Branford Center and East Main Street to the Guilford border. After North Main Street was constructed, maps such as the Price & Lee series did not mark Route 1. Other maps varied and labeled North Main Street as Route 1, others Main Street as Route 1 or sometimes North Main Street as Route 1A. Starting in the 1960s most maps begin to the designate Route 1 as it is today- North Main Street as Route 1, along East Main Street to the Guilford border.

ROUTE 146

Starting at the junction of Main Street and South Main Street east along the shore to the Guilford border

The portion from Damascus to Stony Creek became a state road in 1933[358] and from Damascus to Branford Center a state road in 1955. The entire stretch of Route 146 in Guilford and Branford became a National Register scenic highway in 1996.

RUSSELL STREET

Branford Center, off Main Street to Elm Street, sometimes
   Jay E. Russell Road or Russell Road

The street was put through by the town in 1874[359] on land owned by Jay E. Russell and appears on the 1881 Bird's-Eye map. Russell had extensive land holdings in the Fourth Ward.

RUSTIC ROAD

Brocketts Point, the stretch of road between Howard Avenue and
   Brocketts Point Road, sometimes Laurelwood Road or Rustic Point
   Road
*Map #362 1946 & #399 1947 Lanphier Cove Woods, property
   of Grace LaBarron Lanphier*

The town accepted Laurel Road, Dogwood Drive and Howard Avenue at Lanphiers Cove in 1947.[360] Dogwood Drive, also called Laurel Road, was changed to Rustic Road in 1958.[361]

RUSTIC ROAD

Short Beach
See Rockland Park

SACHEMS LANE AND QUARTERS

Stony Creek

Sachem Lane and Quarters are streets on Money Island developed by Chauncey A. Dickerman in 1869.

SACHEM ROAD

Stony Creek, off Thimble Islands Road to Holly Lane, turns north
   to a dead end, sometimes Gray's Lane

The street was here by 1775 when 14 Sachem Road was built. The street was originally called Rogers Road for the Abraham Rogers family who built the house and was among the early settlers of Stony Creek. The street name was changed in 1958[362] because there was already a Rogers Street in Branford Center. It is named for a Native American sachem. The street is in the National Register Stony Creek Historic District.

SAGAL LOU ROAD

Branford Hills

This was a road leading to the Sagal Lou Farm at Cherry Hill and ran parallel to the current Commercial Parkway. The road has been abandoned and removed.

SAGAMORE COVE ROAD

Pawson Park, off Pawson Road to Sunset Beach Road, sometimes Sagamore Road
Map #1081 1969 First Ecclesiastical Society

The street was built in the early 1900s and appears on the 1936 Price & Lee map but is not named. Earlier maps do not show enough detail. It was a private road owned by the First Ecclesiastical Society and was accepted as a town road in 1968.[363]

SALTONSTALL PARK

Branford Hills
Map #42 1910 land belonging to W. S. & H. L. Chidsey
Map #487 1951 Saltonstall Park section 2, developed by Benjamin D. Pinski

The Chidsey brothers of East Haven built many houses in the western section of Branford. "Roads in Saltonstall Park" were accepted as town roads in 1928.[364] Much of the land was not developed until later when houses were built in the Rose Hill Road area and Pinski Drive.

SALTONSTALL ROAD

Branford Hills
See Hosley Avenue

SANDRA DRIVE

Damascus, off Applewood Road to a dead end
Map #861 1963 Westwood Acres developers Anderson and Drago

The street was accepted as a town road in 1965[365] from Westwood Acres, Inc. and first appears in the 1966 city directory.

The Streets, Alphabetical

SAW MILL ROAD

Stony Creek, off Leetes Island Road and loops back, sometimes Old Saw Mill Road

The saw mill was built in 1832 by Daniel Palmer and the 1852 Whitford and later maps designates "S.M. and D.P." along the road for saw mill and Palmer. The saw mill was later operated by Palmer's grandson Edward S. Palmer. The saw mill was converted to a house in the 1940s.

SCHOOL STREET

Stony Creek, off Leetes Island Road to Thimble Islands Road

The street appears on the 1852 and 1868 maps. It is named for a school built in 1865 that was replaced by another school in 1893, the latter building is now 28 School Street. The street is in the National Register Stony Creek Historic District. A School Street Extension appears on Google maps as an extension of Watrous Avenue but it is not an official town road. This extension appears on earlier maps as Quarry Road.

School Street in Stony Creek showing the former firehouse and town hall.

SCHOOL GROUND ROAD

Off East Main Street to North Branford Road, sometimes
  Schoolground, Schoolgrounds or School Ground Bridge Road
Map #121 1923 School Ground Bridge Road, River Road
Map #786 1961 Bartholomew lands divided into lots by Louis W. Desi

The street appears on the 1852 Whiteford map. A school was located on this road and was moved by 1868 becoming the Paved Street School.[366] The entrance to School Ground Road from East Main Street was reconfigured in the late 20th century and the bridge replaced in 2012.

SCOTCH CAP

The term is an early name for Short Beach. "Land laying in scotch cap" first appears in the town records in 1674.[367]

SCOTCH CAP ROAD

See Short Beach Road

Seaview Avenue in Hotchkiss Grove looking east. Photo by John H. Morton.

SEASTRAND ROAD

Stony Creek, off School Street to a dead end
Map #544 1954 land of Charles O. and M. L. (Mary) Seastrand

The street name first appears on the 1950 Price & Lee map. Before 1950 the street appears as School Street rear. The Seastrand family, natives of Finland, came to Stony Creek in 1904. The street is in the National Register Stony Creek Historic District.

SEAVIEW AVENUE

Hotchkiss Grove
Map #22 1907 property of Emerson M. Hotchkiss

Seaview Avenue appears on the original 1907 plan for Hotchkiss Grove and provided access to the private beach.

SECOND AVENUE

See *Hotchkiss Grove*

SECOND STREET

Branford Hills
See *Carle Road*

SECOND STREET

Indian Neck
See *Dorr Street*

SELDEN AVENUE

Pine Orchard, off Elizabeth Street to a dead end
Map #23 1907 Blackstone Park owned by F. C. Bradley

The street was part of the Blackstone Park development and appears on the 1924 Sanborn map. It was accepted as a town road in 1944[368] from the A. M. Young Company. The origin of the name was not determined.[369]

SEVENTH AVENUE

See *Hotchkiss Grove*

SHADY LANE

Branford Hills, off Briarwood Lane and is a dead end in two directions
Map #792 1961 part of the Briarwood development

The street first appears in the 1970 city directory and was accepted as a town road in 1971.[370]

SHELDON ROAD

Pine Orchard, sometimes Sheldon Place or Sheldon Place Road,
   see Pine Orchard Road
Map #15 1904 Sheldon House property
Map #779 1960 Sheldon House Club, Inc.

The Sheldon House, a summer hotel, was established by Jere Sheldon in 1840 on the bluff overlooking the harbor at Pine Orchard. This location today is east of the Pine Orchard Club. In 1915[371] then owner H. McDonald Allen deeded the stretch of road to the rear of the hotel to the town to be called Sheldon Place Road. This portion of the road appears on the maps as Sheldon Road until 1946 when it became part of Totoket Road. Sheldon Colony Road reappears on the 1964 Price & Lee map until the 1990s. It is no longer an official town road.

SHELLY ANN ROAD

Mill Plain
See Buttermilk Lane

SHEPARDS POINT

See Killams Point

SHEPARD ROAD

Branford Point
See Goodsell Point Road

SHERWOOD STREET

Granite Bay, off Grove Street to Hill Street
Map #64 1915 layout of gas main at Short Beach (Granite Bay)

The street was developed in the early 1900s. It is named for Sherwood Bauer whose family lived at 370 Shore Drive. Jacob Bauer planted many of the pine trees in the area.

SHORE DRIVE
Short Beach
Short Beach Road becomes Shore Drive west of Double Beach Road and becomes Short Beach Road again in East Haven after crossing over the Farm River; originally Main Street, sometimes Dyke Road, Short Beach Road, Elm Terrace

This road was one of the earliest in the Short Beach section of Branford when cottages were built in the 1870s. A small section west of Double Beach Road was built by 1868 leading the house of Virgil U. Cooke. The section from Cooke's house to Pentecost Street was extended in 1875[372] by the town. Part of this latter section from Killams Point west to Midwood Road was known as Dyke Road. The remainder of Shore Drive from Pentecost Street west to the Farm River was improved by the town in 1899.[373]

The street was accepted as a town road in 1930[374] when "all roads in Short Beach used by the public" were accepted as town roads. Shore Drive and Short Beach Road to Route 1 (at West Main Street) were state roads by 1917[375] and were widened and straightened at

Early view of Main Street in Short Beach looking west from Bristol Street.

Damage at Center Beach along Shore Drive during the Hurricane of 1938.

Short Beach Road at West Main Street in 1950. The roads were widened and reconfigured in 1974.

that time. Shore Drive was designated as Route 171 in 1922 and redesignated in 1932 as Route 142. The street was long known as Main Street and the name changed to Shore Drive in 1958[376] running from the East Haven-Branford line to Double Beach Road. Shore Drive becomes Short Beach Road in East Haven, creating confusion. Adding to the confusion Short Beach Road in Branford runs from Double Beach Road to West Main Street. Shore Drive was sometimes also called Short Beach Road and still appears on some maps with one or both names.

The beach along Shore Drive has been known as Center Beach, Hamilton Beach or Page's Cove Beach. The beach just west of Killams Point is not named but sometimes is referred to as Granite Bay Beach.

SHORT BEACH

Short Beach is the most westerly shoreline section of Branford formerly called Scotch Cap. The first year-round house was built in 1849 by Warren Bradley and Short Beach became a summer cottage community shortly after the Civil War.

SHORT BEACH MANOR

See Altman and Berger Streets

SHORT BEACH ROAD

Off West Main Street to the junction of Shore Drive and Double Beach Road; sometimes Scotch Cap Road
Maps #439 & #468 1948 on land developed by Ray U. Plant as part of the Maple Corners

The street was here by 1750 when the Lanfare and Linsley families settled at Double Beach. The street was a state road by 1917.[377] In 1941 the street became part of the State of Connecticut highway system- Route 142. The northern portion of the street was part of Maple Corners developed by Ray U. Plant in 1948.

SHORT ROCKS ROAD
Mill Plain, off Mill Plain Road to Chestnut Street

The section of town known as Short Rocks was first mentioned in the Town Records in 1708 "land above The short Rocks."[378] The area was settled by the Goodrich family by 1750 and in 1899 the Supply Ponds were built by damming the Queach Brook.[379] The road was reconfigured at that time. Houses were built along the street in 1956 as part of the Lakeside development.

SIDE HILL ROAD
Brushy Plain, off Heritage Hill Road to Mountain Top Drive
Map #909 1966 Laurel Hill development, Gargano Construction Co. owner and developer

The street first appears in the 1973 city directory.

Soundview Heights about 1920.

SILVER STREET

Branford Center, off Ivy Street to a dead end

The street first appears on the 1881 Bird's-Eye map and was put through about that time. The street was built to provide housing for employees of the Branford Lock Works.

SIOUX PLACE

Indian Neck
See *Old Pawson Road*

SIXTH AVENUE

See *Hotchkiss Grove*

SMUGGLERS ROAD

Granite Bay
See *Burr Street*

South Main Street looking east from Eades Street in 1933. Photo by Charles A. Blackstone.

SOFFER PLACE

Off Arrowhead Lane to a dead end, sometimes Soffer Lane

The street was accepted as a town road in 1966[380] and first appears in the 1968 city directory. It is named for the Soffer family who developed the property.

SOUNDVIEW HEIGHTS

Indian Neck, off Linden Avenue to a dead end
Map #39 1910 Soundview Heights

The street was developed in 1910 with 28 lots for summer cottages.

SOUTH MAIN STREET

Branford Center, off Main Street to Montowese Street

The street was put through about 1700. South Main Street became part of the Connecticut State Highway system in 1955 and as part of the National Register Route 146 scenic highway in 1996. The street is also in the National Register Branford Center Historic District.

SOUTH MONTOWESE STREET

Indian Neck, off Montowese Street south of the Branford River to the junction of Linden and Sybil Avenues, sometimes lower Montowese Street, Indian Neck Road

Montowese Street was extended south to Indian Neck when a bridge was built across the Branford River in 1791. The entire stretch was called Montowese Street and South Montowese first appears in the 1928 city directory. It was sometimes called Indian Neck Road, lower Montowese Street and is also referred to on one map as Linden Avenue.[381] South Montowese Street was widened in 1899 and became a state road by 1917.[382] It became part of the Connecticut State Highway system in 1955 and as part of the National Register Route 146 scenic highway in 1996. House numbers were changed between 1960 and 1967.

The Streets, Alphabetical |77

A horse and carriage going south from the Montowese Street railroad underpass. Photo by Harry O. Andrews

Indian Neck Avenue at South Montowese Street before a gas station was built at the intersection about 1936.

SOWHEAG PATH

Pawson Park
See Pawson Road

SPICE BUSH LANE

Off Alps Road to a dead end
Map #1533 1979 Spice Hill development, 15 lots

The street was accepted as a town road in 1980[383] and first appears in the 1981 city directory. A spice bush is a native plant.

SPRING COVE ROAD

Pawson Park, off Pawson Road to Ferry Lane, sometimes Spring Cove Lane
Map #705 1950 First Ecclesiastical Society

The street first appears in the 1950 city directory but was here as early as 1930. The street was a private road owned by the First Ecclesiastical Society and was accepted as a town road in 1968.[384]

SPRING LANE

See Zuwalick Lane

SPRING ROAD

Johnsons Point, off Johnsons Point Road to a dead end

The details of the roads at Johnsons Point do not appear on maps until the 1960s. The street was built in 1904 by M. P. Rice of Branford for the Foote family who subdivided the point into lots.

SPRING ROCK ROAD

Pine Orchard, off Pine Orchard Road south to a dead end

The street was put through and lots offered for sale in 1893. It was originally called Blackstone Avenue. The street was accepted as a town road in 1917.[385]

SQUAW BROOK ROAD

Stony Creek, off Thimble Islands Road to Three Elms Road, sometimes Grays Lane, Brainerd Avenue

The street does not appear on the 1852, 1856 or 1868 maps but some of the houses were built shortly afterwards. It appears in the 1895 city directory as Grays Lane and Brainerd Avenue on Map #18. It first appears as Squaw Brook Road on the 1924 Sanborn map. According to tradition it was so named because a squaw fell into the brook.[386] The street is in the National Register Stony Creek Historic District.

STANLEY POINT

Short Beach
See Little Bay Lane

STANNARD AVENUE

Branford Point, off Short Beach Road to Harbor Street

The street was here in the mid-1700s and was the route taken to Branford Point before the bridge was built over the Mill Creek in 1820. The street appears on the 1852 map and was reconfigured or improved by the town in 1878.[387] It is named for Capt. William Stannard of Westbrook who came to Branford about 1870.

STONE STREET

Granite Bay, off Grove Street to Union Street

The street was built by 1902 when Civil War veteran Watson W. Stone built two houses on the street. A proposal to change the street name was rejected in 1975.[388]

STONEGATE DRIVE

Short Rocks, off Short Rocks Road and loops back
Map #664 1968 Lakeside subdivision, owner and developer Frederic Rosenthal

The street first appears in the 1967 city directory and was accepted as a town road in 1969[389] as Lakeside Drive from Anderson-Wilcox, Company. Stonegate is also a condominium complex built in 1974 off Briarwood Lane at Alps Road.

Spring Rock Road looking south showing Hollmann's Waiting Station on the corner. Photo postcard by the Hunter Photo Co. of Madison.

Stannard Avenue in the 1950s taken by Arthur L. Seaburg.

STONEWALL LANE

Off Featherbed Lane to a dead end, sometimes Stone Wall
Map #496 1952 property of John V. and William T. Beazley

The street was accepted as a town road in 1953[390] from John V. and William T. Beazley and first appears in the city directory the same year.

STONY CREEK

Stony Creek is a shoreline community in the eastern part of Branford and was always presumed to be the name for the stream which flows along its border.[391] The name more likely refers to a place near a stream or creek.[392] The name first appears in 1646[393] "…. land at Stony Crick" and was part of the fifth land division granted in 1671. It was settled about 1700 by the Frisbie, Howd, Palmer, Barker, Cook, Rogers, and Hoadley families. After the Civil War, Stony Creek became a popular summer destination. Stony Creek-Thimble Islands is a district on the National Register of Historic Places.

The public dock at Stony Creek showing Burr and Rogers Islands.

STONY CREEK QUARRY ROAD

Stony Creek
See Quarry Road

STONY CREEK ROAD

From the junction of Damascus and Totoket Roads to the junction of Leetes Island and Thimble Islands Roads, see also Damascus Road

The street appears on the 1852 Whiteford map and was the main route to Stony Creek from Damascus. An 1855 deed calls it the new highway. The designation of Stony Creek Road has changed over time and Damascus Road was also called Stony Creek Road or Old Stony Creek Road. The road was improved by the town in 1898 and 1921.

In 1944[394] the town realigned the junction of Leetes Island, Stony Creek, and Thimble Islands Roads. In 1958[395] Stony Creek Road was designated as being from Damascus Road and Totoket Road to Leetes Island Road. The street became part of the Connecticut State Highway- Route 146 in 1962[396] which became a scenic highway in 1996.

SULLIVAN STREET

Branford Center
See Cherry Street

SUMMER ISLAND ROAD

Indian Neck, off Bayberry Lane to a dead end
Map #48 1912 Summer Island

The street was put through in the 1890s and cottages built on land that was part of the Beach family 99-year Pawson Park lease later sub-leased to Frederick Averill. The name Summer Island first appears in an 1898 deed.[397] The name appears as Summer Island Road (Bayberry Lane) on the 1924 Sanborn map. The street was a private road owned by the First Ecclesiastical Society and was accepted as a town road in 1968.[398]

SUMMER ISLAND ROAD EXTENSION

Indian Neck
See Summer Island Road

About 1920 Gurdon Bradley extended Summer Island Road west beyond Sunset Beach Road to the peninsula and dug a lagoon. The name Summer Island Road Extension first appears as a street name on the 1954 zoning map and continues to be on maps in the 1990s. The Town now designates this section as Summer Island Point.

SUMMIT GARDENS

Branford Hills
Map #657 1956 Summit Gardens development by Summit Garden Apartments

Summit Gardens was a proposed development between Matthew Road and Orchard Hill Road much of which did not materialize. Some of the proposed street names were Center Circle, Highland Drive, Sachs Drive, and Summit Drive.

SUNRISE COVE ROAD

Double Beach
Off Double Beach Road to a dead end

The street was developed as a summer camp and most of the cottages were built in the 1950s. Some of the houses are now year-round. It first appears in the 1956 city directory and is a private road.

SUNSET BEACH ROAD

Indian Neck, off Summer Island Road to a dead end in two different directions, sometimes Bayberry Lane

The street was put through by 1900 when cottages on Sunset Beach were built. The street was part of the Beach 99-year Pawson Park lease. Part of the road was called Sunset Lane on the 1924 Sanborn map. The street was a private road owned by the First Ecclesiastical Society and was accepted as a town road in 1968.[399]

SUNSET HILL ROAD

Pine Orchard, off Griffing Pond Road and loops back to Griffing Pond, originally called Round top or Dod's Hill, sometimes Sunset Hill Drive
Map #679 1957 road layout of Sunset Hill, Griffing Pond, and Meadow Wood Roads by the A. M. Young Company

The street was accepted as a town road in 1950[400] from the A. M. Young Company and first appears on the 1953 Price & Lee map. A small section appears on the 1950 Price & Lee map as Old Farm House Road leading to the Hoadley house at 15 Sunset Hill Road.

SUNSET LANE

Indian Neck
See Sunset Beach Road

SUNSET MANOR ASSOCIATION

See Bayview Avenue, Fenway Road, Manor Place, Pawson Road, Sagamore Cove Road, Sunset Beach Road, and Sunset Manor Road

SUNSET MANOR ROAD

Pawson Park, off Pawson Road to Sunset Beach Road
Map #99 1924 land of the Indian Neck Land Co., 24 lots
Map #111 1924 Sunset Manor
Map #1081 1969 First Ecclesiastical Society

The street appears on the 1936 Price & Lee map but is not named. It was originally called Averill Avenue or Road. The street name was changed in 1958[401] because there was already an Averill Place in Branford Center. The street was a private road owned by the First Ecclesiastical Society and was accepted as a town road in 1968.[402]

SURREY LANE

Queach, off Carriage Hill Drive to Coachman Drive
Map #881 1962 Anderson-Wilcox Co.

The street was accepted as a town road in 1966[403] and first appears in the city directory the same year. It was part of the Brookhills, Inc. development, a subdivision called Carriage Hill.

SUSAN DRIVE

Mill Plain
See *Ramblewood Drive*

SVEA AVENUE

Branford Center, off Main Street to a dead end

The property was owned by Charles S. Bradley and he put the street through about 1917. In 1919 Svea Hall was built at 8 Svea Avenue on land leased from Bradley. Svea was the mother of Sweden or the personification of Sweden (Moder Svea). There were many Svea Lodges throughout the country.

SWIFT STREET

Branford Point, off Maple Street becoming West End Avenue

The street appears on the 1852 map as part of Bradley Street. The section between West End Avenue and Maple Street was renamed Swift Street in 1958[404] for the Swift family. Judah Swift came to Branford in 1888 to run the Branford Point Hotel. A portion of the street was developed in 1948 by Ray U. Plant as part of Maple Corners.

SYBIL AVENUE

Indian Neck; South Montowese Street becomes Sybil Avenue at the creek which becomes Limewood Avenue along the water, sometimes Sybil Creek Road

The street was put through about 1840 when the house at 7 Sybil Avenue was built by the Wilford family. The rest of the street was laid out in 1883.[405] The road is named for Sybil or Sibbie's Creek, formerly called Norton's Creek. The origin of the name is unclear, some speculate that Sibben was a local Indian; others claim it is named for Sybil Foote.[406] Until the early 20th century, the creek was wider and deeper allowing boats to reach the bridge at South Montowese Street and Sybil Avenue.[407] Sybil Avenue became part of the Connecticut State Highway- Route 146 in 1955 and as part of the National Register Route 146 scenic highway in 1996.

SYLVAN POINT

Indian Neck, off Indian Neck Avenue along the Branford River

The mixed-use development was built from 1982 to 1986. The area was formerly known as the Pines or Rodden Woods.

SYLVIA STREET

Off East Main Street to a dead end
Map #1977 1959 Sylvia Street, property of Albert Sylvia

The street was accepted as a town road in 1958 and was described as formerly part of Route 1 which was discontinued by the State of Connecticut.[408] The street first appears in the 1960 city directory.

TABOR DRIVE

Off South Montowese Street to Marshall Road

Originally called Little Plain Road, the street was built by 1899 when the Swedish Lutheran Cemetery was established and appears on the 1905 Bird's-Eye view map. By 1931 the street was extended beyond the cemetery. The street name was changed in 1958[409] and named for the new Tabor Lutheran Church which was built in 1957. Part of Tabor Drive was developed in 1955 as the Little Plain subdivision.

Sybil Avenue near the junction of Linden Avenue and South Montowese Street. Photo by Earl Colter.

TAINTOR DRIVE

Branford Center, off South Main Street to Town Hall Drive

Taintor Drive is named for John Taintor who in his will dated August 15, 1699 said "I do give to ye town of Branford part of my homelot... which I do give to sd Towne to build a publick meeting house upon, and to continue for that use unles ye town build elsewhere then the land shall be ye common or what other use ye town see meet."[410] Since that time the Town Records refer to the plot as "ye Towne plot green," "the common," and later "the public green" or "our public green." The road from South Main Street east of the First Congregational Church was named Taintor Drive in 1959 and was previously unnamed.[411]

TAYLOR PLACE

Short Beach, off Shore Drive to Westwood Road, sometimes Taylor Avenue
Map #110 1925 property of Merritt E. Taylor

The street was put through and subdivided by Merritt E. Taylor in 1925 and most of the lots were given to family members. The land originally belonged to the Warren Bradley family. The street first appears in the 1930 city directory and was accepted as a town road in 1936.[412]

TEN ACRES

Branford Point
See Mill Creek Place and Mill Creek Road

TERHUNE AVENUE

Indian Neck, off Indian Neck Avenue to a dead end

The street appears in the 1895 city directory and was built about that time. It was named for Nicholas Terhune and family who came to Branford about 1870. The street was accepted as a town road in 1936[413] from Frederick A. Simpson.

TERRACE AVENUE

Blackstone Acres
See Hawthorne Terrace

THE CUT-OFF

Branford Center
See North Main Street

THE GREENS

Branford Hills, off Florence Road looping back

The Greens is a large condominium complex built beginning in 1975 in several phases. Included are the streets Crosswoods Drive, Emerson Drive, Longfellow Drive, Peddlers Drive, Robert Frost Drive, Thoreau Road, and Walden Lane.

THIMBLE FARMS ROAD

Pine Orchard, off Totoket Road to a dead end
See Juniper Point Road
Map #704 & #752 1958 Thimble Farms, owned and developed by Thimble Farms, Inc.

Ammi Baldwin built a house here in 1847 in the area known as Long Marsh. The street appears on the 1868 Beers map when J. J. Lund was the proprietor of a seashore hotel, later known as the Wybessot House. Thomas B. Doolittle, a telephone pioneer, purchased the property in 1897 and called it Thimble Farms. It does not appear as a named street until the 1965 Price & Lee map and was previously a private drive. The land was developed by Anthony A. Papa in the 1960s.

THIMBLE ISLANDS

Stony Creek

Is a group of islands off the shore of Stony Creek some of which have houses, the earliest built in 1846 on Pot Island. The term Thimble Islands first appears in 1767.[414]

The Streets, Alphabetical

The Weybosett House. Thomas B. Doolittle named the property Thimble Farms.

Thimble Islands Road, formerly called Main Street, looking south along the beach. Photo postcard by Underwood & Underwood.

THIMBLE ISLANDS ROAD

Stony Creek, from the junction of Stony Creek and Leetes Islands Roads and ends at Flying Point Road and Prospect Hill Road, sometimes Thimble Island Road

The street was the main road to the village of Stony Creek which was settled in the early 19th century. Portions of the street have been called various names including Main Street, Brainerd Street, Palmer Road, Flying Point Avenue, Flying Point Road, and Water Street. It was known as Main Street when the name was changed in 1958[415] to eliminate multiple Main Streets in town. The street is in the National Register Stony Creek Historic District.

THIRD AVENUE

Branford Hills
See *Damien Road*

THIRD AVENUE

See *Hotchkiss Grove*

THIRD STREET

Indian Neck

A 1913 map for lots sold at the corner of Pawson Park Road and Linden Avenue refers to 1st Street (Maltby Street), 2nd Street (Dorr Street), and 3rd Street north of Dorr Street. The latter street was never built.

THOMPSON STREET

Off North Branford Road to Flax Mill Road, sometimes Thompson Road

The street is the southern portion of Flax Mill Road and was renamed in 1975 for the Henry G. Thompson Company.

THOREAU ROAD

Branford Hills
See *The Greens*

THREE ELMS ROAD

Stony Creek, off Thimble Islands Road and becomes Squaw Brook Road, sometimes Three Elms Avenue, Elm Street

The street does not appear on the 1868 map but was put through shortly afterwards when Ebenezer J. Coe established the Three Elms Hotel. The road was extended by the town in 1913.[416] The street is in the National Register Stony Creek Historic District.

TIN CAN ALLEY

Stony Creek
See *Watrous Avenue*

TIPPING DRIVE

Off School Ground Road to a dead end
Map #1363 1976 Tipping subdivision

The street was accepted as Tipping Road in 1977[417] and first appears in the 1978 city directory. It is named for owner Leroy Tipping.

TODDS HILL ROAD

Brushy Plain, off North Main Street to Cherry Hill Road

A portion of Todds Hill Road appears on the 1852 Whiteford map and in 1868 only John O'Brien was living here. The street is perhaps named for John Todd, Jr. of New Haven who owned land in this area in the early 1700s. The entrance to Todds Hill Road from North Main Street was reconfigured about 2010.

TOOLE DRIVE

Off South Montowese Street to Indian Neck Avenue
Map #562 1955 Louis A. Festa owner and developer
Map #576 1955 Churchill Realty Co. owner and developer

The street was developed in 1954 by Louis Festa called Toole Estates and the development was soon taken over by Churchill Realty Company. The street was accepted as a town road in 1956[418] from the Churchill Realty Company and appears the same year in the city directory. The land belonged to and the street named for the Thomas Toole family who lived at 15 South Montowese Street.

TOTOKET ROAD

Off Damascus Road to Pine Orchard Road
See Featherbed Lane

A petition to build the road between Damascus and World's End Creek was approved at a town meeting in 1844.[419] The road appears on the 1852 Whiteford map. Until about 1948 Featherbed Lane was called Totoket Road. Starting in 1945 from Featherbed Lane south past Juniper Point and Thimble Farms also became known as Totoket Road and is the name of the road today. This southern portion was previously called Pine Orchard Road and Sheldon Place. Totoket Road became part of the Connecticut State Highway system- Route 146 in 1962[420] and as part of the National Register Route 146 scenic highway in 1996.

There is also a Totoket Road in North Branford which is the name of Brushy Plain Road when it crosses the North Branford border. This road continues north to Forest Road (Route 22) in Northford. Totoket is the name of the Native peoples before the English came and Branford was known as Totoket until the 1660s.

Three Elms Road was named for the three trees that stood in front of the hotel. Photo postcard by Underwood & Underwood.

TOWN HALL DRIVE

The Green, off Main Street to Montowese Street

The street first appears on the 1905 Bird's-Eye map. In 1930, it was called Branford Green Drive.

TOWNER SWAMP ROAD

Off East Main Street to a dead end
See Goldsmith Road and Orchard Lane, sometimes Towner's Hill Road

The road appears on the Guilford 1868 Beers map and is named for the Towner family of Branford who had extensive holdings along East Main Street. Towners Hill appears in the town records in 1692.[421] Richard Towner came to Branford in 1689.

TWEED ROAD

Pine Orchard, off Totoket Road to a dead end
Map #419 1949 land Georgiana Tweed to John H. Tweed, Jr.

The street first appears in the 1962 city directory, but the Tweed family was living here in 1950. John H. Tweed of New York City was an airplane and flight pioneer who came to New Haven in 1905 and started the city's first air service. He was the first manager of the New Haven airport and the airport was renamed for him in 1961.

TYLER AVENUE

Indian Neck, off Limewood Avenue to a dead end

The street first appears on the 1936 Price & Lee map but was here earlier. John R. Tyler was living in this area in 1880 and sold lots at Haycock Point in 1907.

TYLER GREEN ROAD

Branford, off Cedar Street to John Street, now called Main Street, sometimes Tyler Street

The small green between John Street and the Blackstone Memorial Library is called Tyler or Tyler's Green. It is named for Benjamin Tyler (1805-1887) whose house stood on the north side of this green. A small road on the north side first appears on the 1905 Bird's-Eye map and may have been put through the same time as John Street. It appears on the 1924 Sanborn map as Main Street and is not delineated on the Price & Lee maps. During the 1960s it is labeled on some maps as Tyler Street. In 1976, it is referred to as Main Street again, making two Main Streets along this small section west of the Library. Today the buildings have a Main Street address though there is a Tyler Street town sign at the east end of this road. The Town maintains Tyler's Green.

TYLER PLACE

Branford Center
See Eades Street

UNION STREET

Granite Bay, off Grove Street to Forest Street

Granite Bay was developed in the early 1900s and the street appears on a 1910 map. Union streets are named for the Civil War "In the Union there is strength." Watrous Stone and Ira Smith, both early settlers of Granite Bay, were Civil War veterans.

VALLEY STREET

Short Beach, off Farm River Road to a dead end
Map #351 1918 proposed building lots offered by Truman H. Bristol at Short Beach

The street was developed in 1918 and originally named Harrison Street but does not appear until the 1954 zoning map. The street name was changed in 1958[422] because there was already a Harrison Avenue in Branford Center. The street was originally named for Harrison and Truman Bristol, Short Beach land owners and developers.

VALLEY BROOK ROAD

Brushy Plain, off High Meadow Street to Autumn Ridge Road
Maps #863 & 921 1962 Cedar Heights subdivision, Paramont Building Company

The street first appears in the 1967 city directory and was accepted as a town road in 1969.[423]

VALLEY COURT

Branford Center, off Main Street to a dead end and is parallel to Svea Avenue

The street first appears as Martone Drive on the 1965 Price & Lee map. Martone Drive was used through the 1990s but on a 2015 map is called Valley Court. The Martone family came to Branford in 1921, lived at 1171 Main Street and farmed the rear of the property.

VALLEY ROAD

North Branford, off North Branford Road (Branford Road)

Valley Road is in North Branford but a few houses on the southern side of the street are within the bounds of Branford and are listed on Branford's assessors' list.

VEDDER'S POINT ROAD

Stony Creek
See Pleasant Point Road

VENICE STREET

Off East Main Street north to a dead end
Map (no number) 1954 zone change, owner Sante Borsoi

The street was accepted as a town road in 1952[424] from Delos Borsoi and first appears in the 1953 city directory.

VETO STREET

Branford Center, off Main Street to a dead end

The street first appears in the 1895 city directory and was built about that time by M. P. Rice for his new livery stable. The origin of the name is not known, but someone recalled that when a man who worked at the stable appeared before the judge for drunkenness and when asked where he lived, he replied "on Veto Street." That was the first time anyone heard the name and it stuck.[425] Another version is that a man was accused of looking at women's legs as they got off the trolley and he said, "I veto that." Today there are no longer any buildings on Veto Street and it is used as access to parking lots behind Main Street buildings.

VICTOR HILL DRIVE

Brushy Plain, off Brookwood Drive and loops back
Map #911 1965 part of Mountain Top Estates owner & developer J. M. Defelice Construction Co., Inc.

The street first appears in the 1968 city directory.

VICTORIA DRIVE

Damascus, off White Birth Lane to a dead end
Map #802 1961 building lots off Windmill Hill Road, John & Charles Maturo developers

The street first appears in the 1960 city directory and was accepted as a town road in 1962 and an extension in 1969.[426] The street is named for Victoria Maturo, mother of the builders. The Maturo family came to Branford about 1905.

VILLAGE GREEN COURT

Branford Center, off Aceto Street to a dead end
Map #1069 1972 developer Raymond Panico et al

The street was accepted as a town road in 1973[427] and first appears in the 1974 city directory.

VINEYARD ROAD

Off Short Beach Road to a dead end
Map #906 1958 re-subdivision of a portion of Jourdan Farm, section C

The street was accepted as a town road in 1958[428] from Fannie Jourdan et al and first appears in the 1960 city directory.

WAKEFIELD ROAD

Indian Neck, off Pawson Road to Spring Cove Road
Map #68 1915 property at Pawson Park (Wakefield Road area)

This street was developed as part of the Pawson Park summer resort established by Samuel Beach in 1883. The former skating rink is now a private home. The street is named for the Walter Wakefield family. The street was a private road owned by the First Ecclesiastical Society and was accepted as a town road in 1968.[429]

WALDEN LANE

Branford Hills
See *The Greens*

WALLACE AVENUE

Pine Orchard
See *Island View Avenue*

WALLACE ROAD

Stony Creek, off Thimble Islands Road and loops back

The street does not appear on the 1868 Beers map and was probably put through shortly afterwards. It was originally called Maple Road and the name was changed in 1958[430] because there was already a Maple Street in Branford Point. The street is named for the Wallace family. Willoughby Wallace lived on the street and donated the land for a library in Stony Creek. The wetlands here are called The Dike. The street is in the National Register Stony Creek Historic District.

WALLMO ROAD

Stony Creek
See *Holly Lane*

WATERSIDE DRIVE

Pine Orchard, off Club Parkway to Island View Avenue, sometimes Waterside Road

The street was developed by the 1880s and was originally called Giles Avenue probably named for Giles Baldwin. It appears as Waterside Drive on the 1924 Sanborn map.

WATROUS AVENUE

Stony Creek, off Leetes Island Road to School Street

The street was accepted as a town road in 1897[431] by request of Oscar C. Kelsey. It is named for Watrous Howd. The street is in the National Register Stony Creek Historic District.

WAVERLY LANE

Indian Neck
See Creek Court and Waverly Road

WAVERLY ROAD

Indian Neck, off Limewood Avenue to a dead end
Map #92 1921 Waverly Road, property of Frederick L. Averill

The street was developed in 1921 by Frederick L. Averill as part of Waverly Park. The northern part of Waverly Road appears on the 1924 Sanborn map as Waverly Lane. The Waverly Hotel was at the corner of Waverly Road and Limewood Avenue and was built in 1920 on the site of the former picture theater. The Waverly Hotel was destroyed by fire in 1975 and new homes built on the site.

WAVERLY PARK ROAD

Indian Neck, off Waverly Road to a dead end, sometimes Waverly Road
Map #92 1921 Waverly Park, property of Frederick L. Averill

The street was developed in 1921 by Frederick L. Averill and appears on the 1924 Sanborn map.

Waterside Drive showing MacLean's Store and the Pine Orchard Post Office.

WAY PLACE

Indian Neck

The private road appears on Map #411- portion of land leased to Willard Curtis Hyatt at Old Pawson Park Road. It refers to 109 Linden Avenue which was originally the James Way house.

WEIR STREET

Indian Neck, off Indian Neck Avenue to a dead end
Map #47 1911 Weir building lots for sale by William and Robert Foote

The Foote brothers sold the first lot in 1901 on land owned by N. E. Bryan and two houses appear on the 1905 Bird's-Eye map. The street appears on the 1924 Sanborn map as Foote (Weir). The Weirs or the Weirs lot are mention in the town records and a weir is by definition, a low dam built across a river to raise the level of water upstream to regulate its flow, or an enclosure of stakes set in a stream as a trap for fish. The street was extended in 1977 with eight additional lots.[432]

WELLSWEEP ROAD

Off Gould Lane to a dead end
Map #753 1961 developer Anderson-Wilcox Co.

The street was accepted as a town road in 1964[433] from the Anderson-Wilcox Company and first appears in the city directory the same year.

WEST END AVENUE

Off Swift Street to Harbor Street

The street first appears on the 1905 Bird's-Eye view map but is not named. The street is listed in the 1900 through 1909 city directories as "Bradley beyond the railroad." The name West End Avenue first appears in the 1913 city directory. The land was owned and developed by the Malleable Iron Fittings Company.

WEST MAIN STREET

Branford Hills, at the junction of Main Street and North Main Street west to the East Haven border

West Main Street is a 19th century name for the colonial Boston Post Road which became part of Route 1 in 1922. The portion over Branford Hills has been graded many times. By 1895 the term West Main Street was used and houses from Bradley Street west had a West Main Street address. In 1912 West Main Street became a state road from the East Haven line to Branford and the road was improved. The street was re-defined in 1958[434] as running from the East Haven line east to what was then a rotary at North Main Street west of the railroad bridge. Houses between Bradley Street and North Main Street junction which formally had a West Main Street address since 1958 have had a Main Street address. For example, The Harrison House, home of the Branford Historical Society was 112 West Main Street and since 1958 is 124 Main Street.

Branford Hills during the Winter of 1934. Photo by Valdemar T. Hammer

The Streets, Alphabetical

The junction of Main, North Main, and West Main Streets was once called The Pretzel. The roads were reconfigured in 1996.

West Main Street looking west from Rose Hill Road. Lake Saltonstall is on the right. Photo by H. Steinberg.

WEST AVENUE

Stony Creek
See Halls Point Road

WEST POINT PLACE

Stony Creek
See West Point Road

WEST POINT ROAD

Stony Creek, off Thimble Islands Road to a dead end
See also Halls Point Road, sometimes West Avenue

West Point Road was the alternate name of Halls Point Road until 1928. The current street first appears in the 1928 city directory as West Point Place and beginning in 1946 as West Point Road. The name Mariners Lane appears on one document. The street is in the National Register Stony Creek Historic District.

WEST AVENUE

Stony Creek
See West Point Road

WEST SIDE AVENUE

See Hotchkiss Grove

WESTWOOD ROAD

Short Beach
Map #94 & #99 1922 property of William J. Kennedy, lots on Westwood & others

The street was developed by William J. Kennedy on land originally belonging to the Warren Bradley family. The street first appears in the 1928 city directory and is named for Warren Westwood.

WHITE BIRCH LANE

Damascus, off Windmill Hill Road to a dead end
Map #802 1961 building lots off Windmill Hill Road, John & Charles Maturo developers
Map #915 1965 John and Charles Maturo, seven additional lots

The street first appears in the city directory in 1962 and the houses were built by the Maturo Brothers Construction Company. The street was accepted as a town road in 1962[435] and an extension in 1974.

WHITING FARM ROAD

Damascus, off Stony Creek Road to a dead end

The street was accepted as a town road in 1950[436] from the A. M. Young Company and first appears in the 1953 city directory. It was named for Howard M. Whiting, attorney for the A. M. Young Company.

WHORTLEBERRY ROAD

Branford Center, off Cedar Street to a dead end
Map #55 1912 proposed new street, land of John B. Sliney

The street first appears in the 1913 city directory. It was a small street with one house, the home of Arthur Jameson, an officer at the Malleable Iron Fittings Company. The house was torn down and the Cedar Woods Retirement Community at 80 Cedar Street was built in 1986. Whortleberry Road still appears on some contemporary maps. The Whortleberry lot is mentioned in 1786.[437]

WILCOX PLACE

Short Beach
Map #94 & #99 1922 property of William J. Kennedy, lots on Wilcox Place & others

The street was developed by William J. Kennedy on land originally belonging to the Warren Bradley family. The street first appears in the 1928 city directory and is presumed named for Robert Wilcox, husband of the poet Ella Wheeler Wilcox.

WILDWOOD DRIVE

Blackstone Acres, off Pine Orchard Road to a dead end, sometimes Wildwood Road
Map #547 1954 Section One, Blackstone Acres development

The street was accepted as a town road in 1955[438] and an extension accepted in 1956.[439] It was originally named Edgewood Drive and the street name was changed in 1958[440] because there was already an Edgewood Street in Granite Bay. The original plans showed another road coming off Wildwood ending in a cul-de-sac named Rockland Court. The latter was never built.

WILFORD AVENUE

Branford Center, off Montowese Street to Church Street

The street was developed when Charles H. Wilford (who built 14 Wilford Avenue) started selling lots in 1891. The street appears in the 1895 city directory. The street was a "substantial middle-class neighborhood" and the owners were merchants or other professionals. Queen Anne is the predominant architectural style. The street was widened and regraded in 1907 and is in the National Register Branford Center Historic District.

WILFORD ROAD

Indian Neck, off Limewood Avenue to Sybil Avenue
Maps #69, #72 & #513 1916 proposed new road and lots, land of Frederick L. Averill

The lots were sold by Frederick L. Averill of the Indian Neck Land Company as early as 1912 and the street first appears in the 1928 city directory. The street is named for the Samuel Wilford family of 7 Sybil Avenue.

WILLOW ROAD

Branford Center, off East Main Street to a dead end

The street first appears in the 1932 city directory and lots were sold by Howard Bartholomew of 137 East Main Street.

Wilford Avenue about 1900. Photo by Mason Foote Smith

Wilford Road in 1921. Photo by VanDyke Studio

WINDMILL HILL ROAD

Damascus, off East Main Street to Damascus Road

The street appears on the 1852 map and was here as early as 1790 when 86 Damascus Road was built. A windmill once stood at 36 Windmill Hill Road.

WOOD ROAD

Johnsons Point, off Johnsons Point Road and loops back
Map #97 1919 building lots at Johnsons Point, owner William R. Foote

The street was part of the Johnsons Point summer community on land sold by William R. Foote in 1902.

WOODLAND AVENUE

Indian Neck, Hotchkiss Grove Road north of Limewood Avenue
Map #433 1945 road near Hotchkiss Grove, Woodland Avenue

A development north of Hotchkiss Grove Road known as Woodland Terrace by architect and builder Monroe & Monroe for seven new year-round houses was planned in 1928.[441] Woodland Avenue is designated on the 1914 and 1945 map of Hotchkiss Grove and all portions were abandoned and discontinued in 1953.[442]

WOODLAWN AVENUE

Indian Neck, from Melrose Avenue to George Street
Map #73 1918 Branford Gardens, owned and developed by John J. Linsky, 68 lots

The street was accepted as a town road in 1935[443] from John J. Linsky and first appears in the 1936 city directory. It was part of the Branford Gardens development.

WOODSIDE DRIVE

Off Ark Road to a dead end
Map #967 1966 Woodside subdivision by Ernest N. DePoto

The street first appears in the 1969 city directory.

WOODVALE ROAD

Blackstone Acres, off Pine Orchard Road to Riverside Drive
Map #555 & 663 1955 Blackstone Acres section one, Buza, Sturgess & Jockmus Co.

The street was accepted as a town road in 1956[444] and was originally named Ridge Lane. The street name was changed in 1958[445] because there was already a Ridge Road in Stony Creek. An extension of Woodvale was accepted in 1960.[446]

WOODVIEW ROAD

Indian Neck

The street only appears on the Price & Lee maps and directories from 1939 until 1959 off Limewood Avenue north to a dead end just east of Crouch Road. It is now a driveway to a few houses behind Limewood Avenue.

YALE COURT

Short Beach, off Farm River Road to a dead end

The street was developed with a few houses in the 1950s and first appears on the 1954 zoning map.

YALE ROAD

Branford Hills
See Helen Road

YALE STREET OR TERRACE

Branford Hills
See Eli Yale Terrace

YEW COURT

The street first appears in the 1953 city directory off Pine Orchard north to a dead end opposite Oak Hollow Road. It still appears on maps through the 1990s. No houses were ever built and it is no longer a designated road.

YOST DRIVE

Mill Plain

The street first appears in the 1953 city directory off Queach Road west to a dead end. It appears on maps through the 1990s but no houses were ever built and it is no longer a designated road.

YOUNG ROAD

Pine Orchard
See Anchorage Farm Road

YOWAGO AVENUE

Pine Orchard, off Pine Orchard Road south to Selden Avenue

The street was developed by the A. M. Young family in 1909 and is named for members of the family: Young, Warner, and Goss. The southern portion was developed first and the northern section later. The street first appears in the 1936 city directory. It was accepted as a town road in 1944[447] from the A. M. Young Company.

ZUWALICK LANE

Off Leetes Island Road to a dead end, sometimes Zuwalick Terrace
Maps #727 & #768 1958 Old Stony Creek Road, Mary and Genevieve Russell to Henry W. Zuwalick, 14 acres

The street first appears as Spring Lane on the 1950 Price & Lee map and the name was changed in 1958.[448] The Zuwalick family came to Branford in 1888 and still owns the property.

APPENDIX

STREETS NAMED FOR PEOPLE OR FAMILIES

Abbotts	Crouch	Hemingway
Aceto	Damberg	Hoadley
Alex-Warfield	Debra	Hopson
Altman	DeForest	Hosley
Averill	Dorr	Hotchkiss
Ballou	Driscoll	Howard
Barker	Dudley	Howd
Bartholomew	Eades	Isabel
Barton	Echlin	Jackson
Bassett	Elinor	Jefferson
Batrow	Elizabeth	Jeffrey
Beach	Ely	John
Beckett	English	Johnsons
Bennett	Esther	Jourdan
Berger	Etzel	Killams
Birch	Field	Kirkham
Bishop	Florence	Lanphier
Blackstone	Frank	Lavassa
Block	George	Lincoln
Bowhay	Gentile	Linsley
Bradley	Gilbert	MacLean
Brainerd	Goldsmith	Maltby
Brandegee	Goodsell	Marian
Bristol	Gould	Marshall
Brocketts	Griffing	Matthew
Bryan	Halls	McDermott
Buckley	Halstead	McKinnel
Burban	Hammer	Medley
Burr	Hamre	Monroe
Cadwell	Harding	Montgomery
Captains	Harrison	Montowese
Clancy	Hart	Newton
Clark	Hawthorne	O'Brien
Collins	Hazel	Pawson
Corbin	Helen	Palmer

Parish	Selden	Todds Hill
Parker	Sherwood	Toole
Patrick	Soffer	Towner
Pequot	Squaw	Tweed
Pinski	Stannard	Tyler
Piscitello	Stone	Victoria
Plant	Svea	Wakefield
Pompano	Swift	Wallace
Reynolds	Sybil	Watrous
Rice	Sylvia	Westwood
Rogers	Taintor	Whiting
Rose	Taylor	Wilcox
Russell	Terhune	Wilford
Sachem	Thompson	Yowago
Sandra	Thoreau	Zuwalick
Seastrand	Tipping	

Panorama of the Thimble Islands from Flying Point.

STREETS NAMED FOR NATURE

Acorn	Cherry	Forest
Alps	Cherry Hill	Garden
Applewood	Chestnut	Glen
Ash	Cove Terrace	Glendale
Bayberry	Creek	Goat Alley
Bayview	Crescent Bluff	Granite
Bear Path	Curve	Gray Ledge
Beaver	Dogwood	Grove
Beechwood	Double Beach	Harbor
Berry Patch	Edgewood	Harborview
Breezy	Elm	Haycock
Briarwood	Evergreen	Haystack
Brookhills	Fairlawn	Hemlock
Brookwood	Farm River	Hickory
Brushy Plain	Fairview	High Meadow
Buena Vista	Fern	High Plains
Buttermilk	Fir Tree	Highland
Cedar	Flat Rock	Hilltop

Ridge	Seaview	Valley
Ridge Acres	Shady Lane	Vineyard
River	Shore	Waterside
Riverside	Soundview	White Birch
Riverview	Spice Bush	Whortleberry
Rock Pasture	Spring	Wildwood
Rock	Stonewall	Willow
Rockland	Sunrise	Wood
Rocky Ledge	Sunset	
Rolling Hill	Three Elms	

NAMED FOR PLACES OR OBJECTS

Anchorage	Flax Mill	Plymouth
Ark	Flying Point	Prospect Hill
Arrowhead	Hillside	Prospect
Boston Post Road	Home	Saw Mill
Brookhills	Homestead	School
Bridge	Indian Neck	School Ground
Bungalow	Indian Point	Short Beach
Castle Rock	Kidds Cave	Short Rocks
Chapel	Leetes Island	Silver
Church	Long Point	Stony Creek
Cider Mill	Mill Plain	Summer Island
Club Parkway	Monticello	Tabor
Cocheco	North Branford	Thimble
Cottage	Northford	Totoket
Court	Old New England	Town Hall
Damascus	Pine Orchard	Union
Dominican	Pasadena	Venice
East Main	Pavilion	Weir
Eli Yale	Pent	West End
Featherbed	Pentecost	West Point
Fenway	Pine Orchard	Windmill
Ferry	Pleasant Point	Yale

ENDNOTES

1   Many streets in Branford should have an apostrophe 's', such as Hall's Point. Throughout Branford's history the plural possessive for streets has not been used. Historically, consistent grammar and punctuation was not used until after the Civil War.

2   *The Branford Review* August 11, 1960, page 1.

3   Published Annual Town Report ending September 1, 1926 citing Town Meeting May 1, 1926.

4   Leonard Reistetter, Assistant Town Engineer, email to the author, July 10, 2015.

5   *Branford Review* March 15, 1962, page 1 and June 14, 1962, page 1.

6   Town Meeting Records 1926-1951, page 416. See Branford Land Records volume 122, page 204.

7   Town Meeting Records 1951-1967, page 225. See Branford Land Records volume 166, page 154.

8   BERA Bulletin, July 1996, volume 12 #7 (Branford Electric Railway-Shoreline Trolley Museum).

9   Branford Town Records transcription volume II, part 1, page 175; refers to original volume II, page 79.

10   James S. Bradley, age 89, a long-time resident of Short Beach showed Alice Taylor Peterson (my grandmother) where the bars were located along Alps Road in 1936. His father, Warren S. Bradley built the first year-round house in Short Beach in 1849 which still stands at 381 Clark Avenue.

11   Town Meeting Records 1926-1951, page 78. An attempt to have a number of roads in Short Beach accepted was made in 1897 but did not pass.

12   Representative Town Meeting (RTM) Minutes 1967-1976, page 152. See Branford Land Records volume 237, page 487.

13   Maps from the A. M. Young Company are in the archives of the Branford Historical Society.

14   Town Meeting Records 1926-1951, pages 498 & 500. See Branford Land Records volume 135, page 417.

15   Branford Land Records volume 106, page 459 & volume 108, page 25 John Hendrickson to Oscar Forsman and Bertel Uljens. The deeds refer to a 1940 map, "land owned by John S. Hendrickson" on file at the Town Clerk's Office. The map, however, was not found in the map collection.

16   Town Meeting Records 1951-1967, pages 166 & 196.

17   Town Meeting Records 1951-1967, page 200. See Branford Land Records volume 161, page 108.

18   Town Meeting Records 1951-1967, page 632. See Board of Selectmen Minutes April 21, 1970.

19   Town Meeting Records 1951-1967, page 349. See Branford Land Records volume 178, page 85.

20   Town Meeting Records 1951-1967, pages 213 & 294.

21   Town Meeting Records 1926-1951, page 488. See Branford Land Records volume 135, page 410.

22   Branford Land Records volume 4, page 531.

23   Branford Land Record volume 135, page 411.

24   RTM Minutes 1967-1976, page 125.

25   Town Meeting Records 1926-1951, page 488. See Branford Lane Records volume 131, page 216.

26   Delbert Bassett married Nellie Bradley.

27   Board of Selectmen Minutes 1967-1969, February 20, 1968. See Branford Land Records volume 233, page 72.

28   Board of Selectmen Minutes 1967-1969, February 20, 1968. See Branford Land Records volume 233, page 72.

29   RTM Minutes 1976-1986, page 127. See Branford Land Records volume 276, page 39.

30   Town Meeting Records 1926-1951, page 488. See Branford Land Records volume 131, page 215.

31   Branford Town Records transcription volume I, page 76, refers to original volume I, page 82.

32   Town Meeting Records 1926-1951, page 78.

33   Published Annual Town Report ending September 1, 1940 citing Town Meeting July 15, 1940. See Branford Land Records volume 103, page 319.

34   Town Meeting Records 1951-1967, page 201. *The Branford Review* 25 September 1958, page 1.

35   Town Meeting Records 1926-1951, page 78.

36   Town Meeting Records 1926-1951, page 488. See Branford Land Records volume 131, page 214.

37   Town Meeting Records 1951-1967, pages 200 & 206. *The Branford Review* 25 September 1958, page 1.

38   Branford Land Records volume 149, pages 124 & 125.

39   Conversation with Janet (Bartholomew) Strickland Russell, 2016.

40   *The Branford Review* September 16, 1954, page 1. At the time of the 1954 sale the owners were Grace Lanphier of Branford and John and Mark Bishop of Cheshire. The selling price was $65,000.

41   published Annual Town Report citing Town Meeting October 7, 1895. *The Branford Opinion*, June 20, 1896.

42   Published Annual Town Report ending September 15, 1897 citing January 15, 1897 Town Meeting.

43   Old map #43, page 30.

44   Town Meeting Minutes 1951-1967, page 380; *Branford Review*, April 19, 1962, page 1.

45   Branford Land Records volume 164, page 72. The deed is from a court case determining value of the land condemned by the town for highway purposes.

46   *The Old Post Road*, Stewart H. Holbrook, McGraw Hill, New York, 1962.

47   Branford Land Records volume 78, page 411.

48   Map #414 New Haven Railroad land.

49   Town Meeting Records 1951-1967, page 202.

50   Published Annual Town Report ending September 10, 1917. See Branford Land Records volume 67, page 516.

51   Town Meeting Records 1926-1951, page 228.

52   RTM Minutes 1967-1976, page 165.

53   Branford Land Records volume 45, page 3.

54   Branford Town Records December 9, 1667 transcription volume I, page 241, refers to original volume I, page 229. The use of Branford was gradual and was not decided at a town meeting.

55   Branford Town Records transcription volume I, page 12, refers to original volume I, page 13. See Branford Land Records volume 98, page 165.

56   Published Annual Town Report citing Town Meeting November 7, 1918.

57   Town Meeting Records 1926-1951, page 171.

58   RTM Minutes 1967-1976, pages 142 & 219.

59   Janice Plaziak to Jane Bouley, email September 5, 2017.

60   No date was found but probably washed away in the 1920s.

61   Town Meeting Records 1926-1951, page 123.

62   Branford Land Records volume 234, page 138.

63   Town Meeting Records 1951-1967, page 183. See Branford Land Records volume 189, page 230.

64   Town Meeting Records 1926-1951, page 488.

65   Branford Town Records volume 3, page 108.

66   *Branford Review*, April 19, 1962, page 1.

67   Town Meeting Records 1926-1951, page 106. See Branford Land Records volume 88, page 541.

68   Map #28 1909 Ozone Park. Included 26 lots and new roads called Division Avenue and Water Street.

69   *Branford Review* July 12, 1960, page 1.

70   Town Meeting Records 1926-1951, page 78.

71   Notes of Alice Taylor Peterson.

72   Town Meeting Records 1926-1951, page 489. See Branford Land Records volume 131, page 217.

73   Town Meeting Records 1951-1967, pages 550 & 551. See Branford Land Records volume 195, page 183.

74   Branford Town Records transcription volume I, page 83, refers to original volume I, page 75.

75 Town Meeting Records 1926-1951, page 259. See Branford Land Records volume 103, page 240.

76 Town Meeting Records 1951-1967, page 202. *The Branford Review* September 25, 1958, page 1.

77 Town Meeting Records 1951-1967, page 621; RTM Minutes 1967-1976, page 9. See Branford Land Records volume 205, page 264.

78 *Branford Review* July 20, 1967, page 1

79 Branford Land Records, volume 88, page 518.

80 Town Meeting Records 1951-1967, page 289. See Branford Land Records volume 174 and *Branford Review* November 16, 1961, page 1.

81 Town Meeting Records 1951-1967, page 380; *Branford Review,* April 19, 1962, page 1.

82 Town Meeting Records 1951-1967, page 202. *The Branford Review* September 25, 1958, page 1.

83 Town Meeting Records 1951-1967, page 154. See Branford Land Records volume 184, page 188.

84 Branford Town Records transcription volume I, page 92, refers to original volume I, page 98.

85 Published Annual Town Report ending September 15, 1882. The survey appears in Branford Land Records volume 54, page 4.

86 Published Annual Town Report ending September 15, 1892. Branford Land Records volume 45, page 4.

87 *The Supply Pond,* Jane Bouley and Jane Dougherty, 2003, privately printed.

88 Branford Land Records volume 41, page 72.

89 House occupied by a minister.

90 RTM Minutes 1976-1986, page 64.

91 Branford Land Records, volume 25, page 479 and volume 35, page 349.

92 Town Meeting Records 1926-1951, page 78.

93 Town Meeting Records 1951-1967, page 607; RTM Minutes, page 9. See Branford Land Records volume 189, page 232.

94 Town Meeting Records 1926-1951, page 433. See Branford Land Records volume 126, page 374.

95 The Turnpikes of New England, Frederic J. Wood, 1919, Marshall Jones Co., Boston.

96 Board of Selectmen Minutes April 21, 1970.

97   Town Meeting Records 1951-1967, page 201. *The Branford Review* September 25, 1958, page 1.

98   Board of Selectmen Minutes 1967-1969, February 20, 1968. See Branford Land Records volume 233, page 72.

99   Town Meeting Records 1951-1967, page 201. *The Branford Review* September 25, 1958, page 1.

100   Town Meeting Records 1926-1951, page 78.

101   The ownership of Crescent Bluff Avenue has been in court for many years; besides court records see *The New Haven Register* October 7, 2001, page 1 & March 23, 2009, page A1 and *The Sound* October 22, 2009, page 10.

102   RTM Minutes 1967-1976, page 529.

103   Town Meeting Records 1951-1967, page 349. See Branford Land Records volume 178, page 85.

104   Branford Land Records volume 6, page 317.

105   This intersection has been reconfigured several times and was once steeper. 1907- Parting Paths is known as a very dangerous curve with many collisions and near misses. 1913- the old road at Parting Paths was filled in. 1923- a new layout is proposed for Parting Paths. The current configuration with a "T" intersection was completed in 1988.

106   The Poor House was to the rear of about where 67 Damascus Road is today. It was also known as the Poor Farm, Town Farm or the Alms House.

107   Town Meeting Records 1951-1967, page 202.

108   Branford Land Records volume 103, page 319.

109   Town Meeting Records 1951-1967, page 202. *The Branford Review* September 25, 1958, page 1.

110   RTM Minutes 1967-1976, page 142.

111   Town Meeting Records 1951-1967, page 212. See Branford Land Records volume 163, page 227.

112   Town Meeting Records 1951-1967, page 191. See Branford Land Records volume 159, page 160 & 468.

113   Town Meeting Records 1926-1961, page 421. See Branford Land Records volume 125, page 440.

114   Town Meeting Records 1951-1967, page 154.

115   RTM Minutes 1967-1976, page 219.

116   Town Meeting Records 1951-1967, page 202. *The Branford Review* September 25, 1958, page 1.

117   Board of Selectmen Minutes 1967-1969, February 20, 1968. See Branford Land Records volume 233, page 72.

118   Published Annual Town Report ending September 1, 1937 citing Town Meeting October 12, 1936. See Branford Land Records volume 98, page 250 and volume 103, page 221.

119   Branford Town Records transcription volume I, page 138; refers to original volume I, page 143.

120   Town Meeting Records 1951-1967, page 206.

121   Published Annual Report ending September 10, 1906.

122   Town Meeting Records 1926-1951, page 488. See Branford Land Records volume 135, page 410.

123   Town Meeting Records 1951-1967, page 202. See Branford Land Records volume 135, page 410. *The Branford Review* September 25, 1958, page 1. The addition of Eli to the street name implies a connection to Yale University which is incorrect. Yale was a Ballou family name.

124   Published Annual Town Report citing Town Meeting October 14, 1901 "a new road between Crescent Bluff and Hotchkiss Grove is postponed."

125   Published Annual Town Report citing Town Meeting October 4, 1920.

126   Published Annual Town Report ending September 10, 1917, page 149.

127   Town Meeting Minutes 1951-1967, page 380; *Branford Review*, April 19, 1962, page 1.

128   The 1902 map is at Town Hall prepared by A. William Sperry and refers to Monroe Place ending at Brown's Wharf. A deed was never recorded.

129   Town Meeting Records 1951-1967, page 356.

130   Town Meeting Records 1926-1951, page 167. See Branford Land Records volume 95, page 339.

131   Town Meeting Records 1926-1951, page 78.

132   Town Meeting Records 1951-1967, page 201. *The Branford Review* September 25, 1958, page 1.

133   Town Meeting Records 1951-1967, page 202. *The Branford Review* September 25, 1958, page 1.

134   Board of Selectmen Minutes 1967-1969, February 20, 1968. See Branford Land Records volume 233, page 72.

135   RTM Minutes 1967-1976, page 142.

136   Board of Selectmen Minutes 1967-1969, February 20, 1968. See Branford Land Records volume 233, page 72.

137   Branford Land Records volume 146, page 321.

138   Branford Land Records volume 135, page 411.

139   RTM Minutes 1967-1976, page 40.

140   Branford Land Records volume 73, page 510.

141   Interview with Phyllis (Ceccolini) Cooke in 2008. Flat Rock Road is mentioned in the Town Meeting Minutes 1926-1951, page 216 referring to Branford Land Records volume 75, page 5.

142   Also called High Rock Road in the 1932 Annual Town Report.

143   Branford Land Records volume 7, page 400.

144   RTM Minutes 1967-1976, page 381.

145   Conversation with Joseph Bahnsen of 101 North Branford Road in 1986. He said the path was always called Flax Mill Road.

146   RTM Minutes 1967-1976, page 381.

147   Town Meeting Records 1951-1967, page 213.

148   *Branford Review* November 16, 1961, page 1.

149   Town Meeting Records 1951-1967, page 348.

150   RTM Minutes 1967-1976, page 165.

151   Published Annual Town Report ending September 10, 1921 citing a Town Meeting dated February 6, 1869 and Branford Land Records, volume 28, page 391.

152   Published Annual Town Reports citing Town Meeting October 2, 1905. See Branford Land Records volume 54, page 570.

153   Published Annual Town Reports ending September 10, 1910 and 1912 citing Town Meeting January 31, 1911.

154   Branford Town Records transcription volume I, page 29; refers to original volume I, page 22.

155   Sylvan Point was formerly known as Rodden's Woods named for the Stephen Rodden family. Frank Street may be named for son Francis Rodden.

156   Town Meeting Records 1926-1951, page 167. See Branford Land Records volume 95, page 337.

157   Town Meeting Records 1926-1951, page 167.

158   Town Meeting Records 1951-1967, page 201. *The Branford Review* September 25, 1958, page 1.

159   Town Meeting Records 1926-1951, page 464. See Branford Land Records volume 134, page 183.

160   *The Branford Review* February 8, 1951.

161   Town Meeting Records 1926-1951, page 78.

162   Town Meeting Records 1926-1951, page 78.

163   Map #272 1940, property of Frederic M. Meng.

164   Town Meeting Records 1926-1951, page 364.

165   RTM Minutes 1976-1986, page 44.

166   Town Meeting Records 1926-1951, pages 464. See Branford Land Records volume 128, page 402 and volume 135, page 415.

167   Town Meeting Records 1951-1967, pages 201 & 206.

168   Published Annual Town Report ending September 10, 1906 citing Town Meeting August 23, 1905 and October 9, 1905. See Branford Land Records volume 54, pages 5 & 570.

169   Town Meeting Records 1951-1967, page 201. *The Branford Review* September 25, 1958, page 1.

170   Halstead died in 1955. There was also a William R. Halstead, an early summer resident.

171   Town Meeting Records 1926-1951, page 426 & 430.

172   Town Meeting Records 1926-1951, page 292. See Branford Land Records volume 103, page 419.

173   Town Meeting Records 1951-1967, pages 206. *The Branford Review* September 25, 1958, page 1.

174   Published Annual Town Report ending September 1, 1926 citing Town Meeting October 12, 1925.

175   Published Annual Town Report ending September 16, 1897 citing Town Meeting October 5, 1896.

176   Town Meeting Records 1951-1967, page 294. See Branford Land Records volume 172, page 614.

177   *The History of Haycock Point*, Howard Tryon, 1962, typescript.

178   Town Meeting Records 1951-1967, page 349. See Branford Land Records volume 178, page 85.

179   Town Meeting Records 1951-1967, page 202. *The Branford Review* September 25, 1958, page 1.

180   Perhaps named for Peter Donadio's sister Helen.

181   A 1907 probate record calls this section near Bayberry Lane-Cedar Ridge.

182   Town Meeting Records 1951-1967, page 201. *The Branford Review* September 25, 1958, page 1.

183   Branford Land Records volume 78. page 308.

184 Board of Selectmen Minutes 1967-1969, February 20, 1968. See Branford Land Records volume 233, page 72.

185 Town Meeting Records 1951-1967, page 349. See Branford Land Records volume 178, page 85.

186 Town Meeting Records 1926-1951, page 488. See Branford Land Records volume 138, page 528.

187 RTM Minutes 1967-1976, page 56. See Branford Land Records volume 189, page 567.

188 *Branford Review* August 19, 1965, page 1.

189 RTM Minutes 1967-1976, page 374.

190 Branford Land Records volume 103, page 71.

191 Town Meeting Records 1926-1951, pages 201, 204, 209 & 214. See Branford Land Records volume 103, page 42.

192 Branford Land Records volume 131, page 381.

193 Branford Land Records volume 56, page 161.

194 Branford Town Records, volume 1, page 106.

195 Shows the streets and lots at Hotchkiss Grove.

196 An attempt to make the streets public by the town failed in a court case in 1940. The residents established their own district in 1989.

197 Most maps use the numerical designation, the town and signs posted by the Hotchkiss Grove Association spell the out the numbers.

198 Town Meeting Records 1926-1951, page 421. See Branford Land Records volume 125, page 438.

199 Town Meeting Records 1951-1967, page 200.

200 RTM Minutes 1967-1976, page 374. See Branford Land Records volume 264, page 714.

201 The street does not appear on the 1881 Bird's-Eye map. 77 Indian Neck Avenue was built in 1887.

202 Published Annual Town Report ending September 10, 1900 citing Town Meeting August 18, 1900. See Branford Land Records volume 50, pages 257 & 258.

203 Town Meeting Records 1951-1967, page 202. *The Branford Review* September 25, 1958, page 1.

204 Published Annual Town Report ending September 21, 1876.

205 Branford Land Records volume 13, page 119.

206 Town Meeting Records 1951-1967, page 401.

207 Town Meeting Records 1926-1951, page 78.

208 *The Branford Review*, September 28, 1955, page 1.

209 Owens Real Estate, obituary of D. William Owens, Jr., *New Haven Register*, August 28, 2017, page 3.

210 Town Meeting Records 1951-1967, page 213.

211 Town Meeting Records 1951-1967, page 225. See Branford Land Records volume 166, page 181.

212 *Branford Review* March 29, 1962, page 1- Fifty lots at Knollwood planned, each owner will build their own custom house.

213 Branford Land Records volume 195, page 178. The road was not accepted by the RTM in 1964- *Branford Review* March 12, 1964, page 1.

214 Town Meeting Records 1926-1951, page 488. See Branford Land Records volume 122, page 550.

215 Town Meeting Records 1926-1951, page 497.

216 Town Meeting Records 1926-1951, page 445. See Branford Land Records volume 126, page 635.

217 Town Meeting Records 1951-1967, page 201. *The Branford Review* September 25, 1958, page 1.

218 Various spellings are in the records- Lanfare, Lanfair, Lanfaer, Lanphier, Lamphere.

219 RTM Minutes 1967-1976, page 523.

220 Conversation with Louis Lavassa, 1984. See Branford Land Records volume 74, page 187.

221 Published Annual Town Report ending September 10, 1906.

222 Town Meeting Minutes 1926-1951, page 135.

223 1954 Planning & Zoning map, proposed street name changes.

224 map #360 1946

225 Town Meeting Records 1926-1951, page 76. Another portion of the street was accepted as a town road in 1935 from Minnie Mory. See Branford Land Records volume 95, page 351.

226 Branford Land Records volume 105, pages 343 & 345

227 Branford Land Records volume 108, page 141.

228 Board of Selectmen Minutes 1967-1969, February 20, 1968. See Branford Land Records volume 233, page 72.

229 Published Annual Town Report ending September 20, 1882. See Branford Land Records 1896 volume 49, page 235 correcting the street line.

230 Branford Land Records volume 103, page 261.

231 Town Meeting Records 1926-1951, page 488. See Branford Land Records volume 131, page 214.

232   Town Meeting Records 1951-1967, page 200. *The Branford Review* September 25, 1958, page 1.

233   Town Meeting Records 1926-1951, page 78.

234   Branford Town Records transcription volume I, page 245; refers to original volume I, page 236.

235   Streets such as Little Plain Road were used to access the salt meadows to harvest salt hay, used as fertilizers on the fields.

236   Town Meeting Records 1951-1967, page 349. See Branford Land Records volume 178, page 85.

237   Town Meeting Records 1951-1967, page 201. *The Branford Review* September 25, 1958, page 1.

238   Town Meeting Records 1951-1967, page 202.

239   Town Meeting Records 1951-1967, page 201. *The Branford Review* September 25, 1958, page 1.

240   Board of Selectmen Minutes 1967-1969, February 20, 1968. See Branford Land Records volume 233, page 72.

241   Town Meeting Records 1951-1967, page 201. *The Branford Review* September 25, 1958, page 1.

242   Board of Selectmen Minutes 1967-1969, February 20, 1968. See Branford Land Records volume 233, page 72.

243   Town Meeting Book A, page 92. Town Meeting July 9, 1855.

244   Town Meeting Book A, page 100. Town Meeting May 31, 1856 a tax levied to pay for a new public road near the Railroad Depot to the Scotch Cap Road near the dwelling house of Samuel E. Linsley. Linsley lived at the north corner of today's Maple Street and Short Beach Road.

245   Town Meeting Minutes 1926-1951, page 321.

246   Town Meeting Records 1951-1967, page 56 & 57.

247   *The Branford Review* October 19, 1961.

248   Town Meeting Records 1951-1967, page 550. See Branford Land Records volume 195, page 175.

249   Branford Land Records volume 135, page 410. See Branford Land Records volume 135, page 410.

250   Town Meeting Records 1951-1967, page 166. See Branford Land Records volume 151, page 133.

251   Town Meeting Records 1926-1951, page 228. Refers to a 1926 map, developers Ideal Home Company, Inc.

252   Town Meeting Records 1926-1951, page 488.

253   Town Meeting Records 1926-1951, page 464. See Branford Land Records volume 128, page 401.

254   Published Annual Town Report ending September 15, 1895.

255   Published Annual Town Report ending September 15, 1895.

256   Town Meeting Records 1951-1967, page 166. See Branford Land Records volume 157, page 132.

257   Town Meeting Records 1951-1967, page 206.

258   Town Meeting Records 1951-1967, pages 154 & 206. See Branford Land Records volume 157, page 129.

259   Town Meeting Records 1926-1951, page 167.

260   Town Meeting Records 1926-1951, page 488.

261   RTM Minutes 1967-1976, page 139. See Branford Land Records volume 165, page 585;

262   Town Meeting Records 1926-1951, page 289.

263   Town Meeting Records 1926-1951, page 289.

264   Transcription volume I, page 12 citing original volume I, page 13.

265   Transcription volume I, page 88 citing original volume I, page 94.

266   *The Branford Review* April 14 & 28, 1960.

267   Town Meeting Records 1951-1967, page 349. See Branford Land Records volume 178, page 85.

268   Town Meeting Records 1951-1967, page 191. See Branford Land Records volume 159, page 454.

269   Branford Land Records volume 190, page 385.

270   Town Meeting Records 1926-1951, page 166. See Branford Land Records volume 95, page 336.

271   His 1862 probate describes his house on Monroe Street (Branford Probate volume 3, page 145 & 173).

272   Published Annual Town Report ending September 16, 1880. See Branford Land Records volume 45, page 8.

273   Board of Selectmen Minutes 1967-1969, February 20, 1968. See Branford Land Records volume 233, page 72.

274   Published Annual Town Report ending September 10, 1917, page 149.

275   Town Meeting Records 1951-1967, page 202. *The Branford Review* September 25, 1958, page 1.

276   Town Meeting Records 1951-1967, pages 200 & 201.

277   No explanation or record was found as to why the house numbers were changed.

278   *The Branford Review* April 9, 1931; December 10, 1931; and September 8, 1932.

279   Branford Land Records volume 93, page 374.

280   Town Meeting Records 1926-1951, page 167; the name was proposed by Earle V. Barker.

281   Town Meeting Records 1951-1967, page 214. See Branford Land Records volume 163, page 228.

282   Town Meeting Records 1951-1967, page 213. See Branford Land Records volume 159, page 468.

283   Town Meeting Records 1951-1967, page 550. See Branford Land Records volume 195, page 181.

284   RTM Minutes 1967-1976, page 142.

285   Town Meeting Records 1951-1967, page 200. See Branford Land Records volume 161, page 255.

286   Town Meeting Records 1926-1951, page 433

287   Town Meeting Records 1951-1967, pages 73, 167, 213 & 338. See Branford Land Records volume 177, page 54.

288   Board of Selectmen Minutes 1967-1969, February 20, 1968. See Branford Land Records volume 233, page 72.

289   Published Annual Town Report ending September 20, 1882.

290   Published Annual Town Report ending September 10, 1915 citing Town Meeting September 14, 1914.

291   Town Meeting Records 1951-1967, page 289.

292   Town Meeting Records 1951-1967, pages 405 & 449.

293   Town Meeting Records 1951-1967, page 184.

294   Notes of Alice Taylor Peterson, in the possession of the author.

295   Town Meeting Records 1951-1967, page 73. See Branford Land Records volume 146, page 79.

296   Town Meeting Records 1951-1967, page 154.

297   *The Branford Review* October 11, 1951, page 5 and December 27, 1951, page 3.

298   Town Meeting Records 1951-1967, pages 632 & 634.

299   *Shore Line Times* May 10, 1900.

300   Town Meeting Records 1926-1951, page 107. See Branford Land Records volume 88, page 543.

301   Branford Land Records volume 152, page 217.

302   Published Annual Town Report ending September 10, 1922 citing Town Meeting June 19, 1922.

303   Town Meeting Records 1926-1951, page 107. See Branford Land Records volume 88, page 542.

304   Town Meeting Records 1951-1967, page 621. See Branford Land Records volume 190, page 660-666. The road was not accepted by the RTM in 1964- *Branford Review* March 12, 1964, page 1.

305   Branford Land Records volume 90, page 399 estate of Julius Kraffert to Robert Patrick.

306   Branford Land Records volume 9, page 34 refers to Paved Street so called.

307   Town Meeting Records 1951-1967, page 631.

308   RTM Minutes 1967-1976, page 40.

309   *The Branford Review* April 21, 1960, page 1.

310   RTM Minutes 1967-1976, pages 19, 23 & 24.

311   Board of Selectmen Minutes 1967-1969, February 20, 1968. See Branford Land Records volume 233, page 72. The land record names the streets and refers to the 1958 maps.

312   Board of Selectmen Minutes 1967-1969, February 20, 1968. See Branford Land Records volume 233, page 72.

313   Board of Selectmen Minutes 1967-1969, February 20, 1968. See Branford Land Records volume 233, page 72.

314   Published Annual Town Report ending September 10, 1913.

315   Town Meeting Records 1926-1951, page 122.

316   Branford Town Records transcription volume 2, part 2, page 23 citing original volume 2, page 9.

317   RTM Minutes 1976-1986, page 127.

318   Branford Town Records transcription volume I, page 249, refers to original page 249.

319   For a history of the development of Pine Orchard see The Pine Orchard Shore: A Brief History and a Glimpse at the Summer of 1916, John B. Kirby, Jr., 1981, privately printed.

320   The section through Pine Orchard was called this by the children because of the hemlocks which lined both sides of the street. Interview with Natica Goss Jones in 2001.

321   Map #975 1962 Old Town Road, Abalin Kennels, 3.05 acres

322   Published Annual Town Report ending September 15, 1897 citing Town Meeting January 19, 1897.

323   Town Meeting Records 1951-1967, page 206.

324   Town Meeting Records 1951-1967, page 380; *Branford Review,* April 19, 1962, page 1.

325   RTM Minutes 1967-1976, page 40.

326   Town Meeting Records 1951-1967, page 632.

327   Town Meeting Records 1926-1951, page 491 & 492.

328   Town Meeting Records 1951-1967, page 55. See Branford Land Records volume 146, page 90.

329   Town Meeting Records 1951-1967, page 154. See Branford Land Records volume 146, page 549.

330   Branford Land Records volume 16, page 227.

331   Town Meeting Records 1926-1951, page 488 and 1951-1967, page 632. See Branford Land Records volume 146, page 322 and volume 210, page 220.

332   Branford Land Records volume 33, page 173. Map #539 shows early lot owners.

333   Published Annual Town Report ending September 10, 1903 citing Town Meeting March 31, 1903 .

334   Branford Land Records volume 93, pages 569-572 & 590.

335   Branford Town Records January 5, 1679, volume 1, 146.

336   Town Meeting Records 1951-1967, pages 550. See Branford Land Records volume 187, page 321 and volume 195, page 183.

337   Branford Land Records volume 14, page 260.

338   Conversation with Luther Harrison in the 1970s who grew up on Flat Rock Road. It is possible it is named for the reddish tint of the granite in the area.

339   RTM Minutes 1976-1986, page 127.

340   Town Meeting Records 1951-1967, page 441. See Branford Land Records volume 182, pages 437, 439 & 441.

341   Town Meeting Records 1926-1951, page 488. See Branford Land Records volume 135, page 413.

342   Maps #1422 & #1426.

343   Town Meeting Records 1951-1967, page 338 and RTM Minutes 1976-1986, page 2. See Branford Land Records volume 131, page 403, volume 146, page 320, and volume 177, page 54.

344   Board of Selectmen Minutes 1967-1969, February 20, 1968. See Branford Land Records volume 233, page 72.

345   Town Meeting Records 1951-1967, page 213. See Branford Land Records volume 159, page 468.

346   Town Meeting Records 1951-1967, page 298. See Branford Land Records volume 172, page 614.

347   Board of Selectmen Minutes 1967-1969, February 20, 1968. See Branford Land Records volume 233, page 72.

348   Map #196 1914

349   RTM Minutes 1967-1976, page 142.

350   Town Meeting Records 1951-1967, page 154. See Branford Land Records volume 146, page 550.

351   Published Annual Town Report ending September 20, 1880. Rock Pasture appears in the records by 1783.

352   Branford Land Records volume 33, page 221 and volume 33, page 296.

353   Town Meeting Records 1951-1967, page 154.

354   Town Meeting Records 1951-1967, page 201. *The Branford Review* September 25, 1958, page 1.

355   Branford Land Records volume 103, page 71.

356   Town Meeting Records 1926-1951, pages 34 & 35.

357   Branford Land Records volume 122, page 550.

358   Town Meeting Records 1926-1951, pages 129 & 135.

359   Published Annual Town Report ending September 20, 1874 and September 21, 1876.

360   Town Meeting Records 1926-1951, page 421. See Branford Land Records volume 175, page 440.

361   Town Meeting Records 1951-1967, page 201. *The Branford Review* September 25, 1958, page 1.

362   Town Meeting Records 1951-1967, page 202. *The Branford Review* September 25, 1958, page 1.

363   Board of Selectmen Minutes 1967-1969, February 20, 1968.

364   Town Meeting Minutes 1926-1951, page 35.

365   Branford Land Records volume 199, page 147.

366   The Paved School, later 10 Leetes Island Road, was converted to a house in 1917 and torn down in 1985. It is now the site of the Super Stop & Shop grocery store.

367   Branford Town Records transcription, volume I, page 143, refers to original volume I, page 147.

368   Town Meeting Minutes 1926-1951, page 354. See Branford Land Records volume 116, pages 419-425.

369   There are no entries in the land record index for the last name Selden. Several of the streets in Blackstone Park were named by Frederick C. Bradley who wintered in Pasadena, California. There is a Selden Pass along the John Muir Trail but it is not located near Pasadena.

370   RTM Minutes 1967-1976, page 142.

371   Branford Land Records volume 70, page 249.

372   Published Annual Town Report ending September 21, 1875, page 22.

373   Old map #20 proposed layout of highway at Short Beach by the Selectman.

374   Town Meeting Records 1926-1951, page 78.

375   Published Annual Town Report ending September 10, 1917, page 149.

376   Town Meeting Records 1951-1967, page 201. *The Branford Review* September 25, 1958, page 1.

377   Published Annual Town Report ending September 10, 1917, page 149.

378   Branford Town Records transcription volume 2, part 2, page 689 citing original volume 2, page 342.

379   The Supply Pond, Jane P. Bouley & Jane Dougherty, 2004, privately printed.

380   Town Meeting Records 1961-1967, page 631.

381   Map #416 1948.

382   Published Annual Town Report ending September 10, 1917, page 149.

383   Branford Land Records volume 316, page 307 and volume 313, page 532.

384   Board of Selectmen Minutes 1967-1969, February 20, 1968. See Branford Land Records volume 233, page 72.

385   Published Annual Town Report ending September 10, 1917 citing Town Meeting June 16, 1917.

386   Connecticut Place Names, Arthur H. Hughes and Morse S. Allen, The Connecticut Historical Society, 1976, page 38 citing History of Stony Creek by McKenzie, page 6.

387   *The Branford News* May 24, 1878.

388   RTM Minutes 1967-1976, page 462.

389   Branford Land Records volume 211, page 63. See Branford Land Records volume 221, page 63.

390   Town Meeting Minutes 1951-1967, page 73. See Branford Land Records volume 146, page 138.

391   A Brief History of Stony Creek, Gertrude Farnham McKenzie, New Haven, Van Dyck & Company, Inc., page 6. References do not refer to the stream being called Stony Creek.

392   From Oiockcommock to Hoadley's Creek: A Topsy-Turvy Tale of the Guilford-Branford Coastal Boundary, Nona Bloomer, typescript, 2017.

393   Branford Town Records transcription volume I, page 3 citing original volume I, page 2.

394   Town Meeting Minutes 1926-1951, page 355.

395   Town Meeting Records 1951-1967, page 202.

396   Town Meeting Minutes 1951-1967, page 380; *Branford Review*, April 19, 1962, page 1.

397   Summer Island, A Century of History and Nostalgia, Phyllis Palmer and Sally D'Amato, 1993, Anchor Press citing Branford Land Records volume 49, page 512.

398   Board of Selectmen Minutes 1967-1969, February 20, 1968. See Branford Land Records volume 233, page 72.

399   Board of Selectmen Minutes 1967-1969, February 20, 1968. See Branford Land Records volume 233, page 72.

400   Town Meeting Records 1926-1951, page 498 & 500. See Branford Land Records volume 135, page 415.

401   Town Meeting Records 1951-1967, page 200. *The Branford Review* September 25, 1958, page 1.

402   Board of Selectmen Minutes 1967-1969, February 20, 1968. See Branford Land Records volume 233, page 72.

403   Town Meeting Records 1951-1967, page 607.

404   Town Meeting Records 1951-1967, page 201. *The Branford Review* September 25, 1958, page 1.

405   Town Meeting Records 1926-1951, pages 185 & 188. See Branford Land Records volume 35, page 500.

406   The latter attribution is in the notes of Eugenia Bradley, in the collection of the Branford Historical Society. Sybil Foote (1765-1843) was the daughter of Nathaniel & Sarah (Beers) Foote.

407   My uncle, born in 1917, remembered as a child sloops and small schooners reaching the bridge.

408   Town Meeting Records 1951-1967, page 206.

409   Town Meeting Records 1951-1967, page 206. *The Branford Review* September 25, 1958, page 1.

410   *The First Church and Society of Branford, Conn.* by Rev. J. Rupert Simonds, 1919 history, New Haven, Tuttle, Morehouse & Taylor Co.

411   Town Meeting Records 1951-1967, page 225. *The Branford Review* July 29, 1959, page 1.

412   Town Meeting Records 1926-1951, page 181. See Branford Land Records volume 98, page 208.

413   Town Meeting Records 1926-1951, page 181. See Branford Land Records volume 95, page 114.

414   Branford Land Records volume 9, page 43.

415   Town Meeting Records 1951-1967, page 201. *The Branford Review* September 25, 1958, page 1.

416   Published Annual Town Report citing Town Meeting February 6, 1913.

417   RTM Minutes 1976-1986, page 96. See Branford Land Records volume 297, page 258.

418   Town Meeting Records 1951-1967, page 154. See Branford Land Records volume 146, page 579.

419   Town Meeting Book A, pages 24 & 25. Town Meeting March 21, 1844.

420   Town Meeting Minutes 1951-1967, page 380; *Branford Review*, April 19, 1962, page 1. The 1902 Annual Report calls the road from the Pine Orchard depot to the Pine Orchard post office a state road.

421   Branford Town Records transcription volume I, page 106, refers to original volume I, page 108.

422   Town Meeting Records 1951-1967, page 201. *The Branford Review* September 25, 1958, page 1.

423   RTM Minutes 1967-1976, page 56. See Branford Land Records volume 189, page 567.

424   Branford Land Records volume 131, page 441.

425   *Branford Review* September 11, 1947, page 5.

426   Town Meeting Records 1951-1967, page 441; RTM Minutes 1967-1976, page 40. See Branford Land Records volume 160, page 167; volume 182, pages 437, 439 & 441; and volume 222, page 573.

427   RTM Minutes 1967-1976, page 353.

428   Town Meeting Records 1951-1967, page 213. See Branford Land Records volume 162, page 477.

429   Board of Selectmen Minutes 1967-1969, February 20, 1968. See Branford Land Records volume 233, page 72.

430   *The Branford Review* September 25, 1958, page 1.

431   Published Annual Town Report ending September 16, 1897 citing Town Meeting July 1, 1897.

432   Map #1374 owner and developer Robert Bailey.

433   Town Meeting Records 1951-1967, page 550. See Branford Land Records volume 195, page 185.

434   Town Meeting Records 1951-1967, page 202. See Branford Land Records volume 182, pages 437, 439 & 441.

435   Town Meeting Records 1951-1967, page 449; RTM Minutes 1967-1976, page 435

436   Town Meeting Records 1926-1951, pages 498 & 500. See Branford Land Records volume 135,

   page 416.

437   Branford Land Records, volume 11, page 58.

438   Town Meeting Records 1951-1967, page 109.

439   Town Meeting Records 1951-1967, page 154.

440   Town Meeting Records 1951-1967, page 201. *The Branford Review* September 25, 1958, page 1.

441   *Branford Review,* April 19, 1928, page 1. It does not appear the development was built.

442   Town Meeting Records 1951-1967, page 52.

443   Town Meeting Records 1926-1951, page 167. See Branford Land Records volume 95, page 337.

444   Town Meeting Records 1951-1967, page 191. See Branford Land Records volume 159, page 468.

445   Town Meeting Records 1951-1967, page 202. *The Branford Review* September 25, 1958, page 1.

446   Town Meeting Records 1951-1967, page 298. See Branford Land Records volume 172, page 614.

447   Town Meeting Minutes 1926-1951, page 354. See Branford Land Records volume 116, pages 419-425.

448   Town Meeting Records 1951-1967, page 202. *The Branford Review* September 25, 1958, page 1.

BIBLIOGRAPHY

Ayres, Harral, *The Great Trail of New England: The Old Connecticut Path*, Meador Publishing Co., 1940.

Baker, Robert B., "Mystery Map of Branford," *Branford Review*, July 30, 1997, page 6.

Bouley, Jane, "Boston Post Road," *Branford Review*, November 18, 1992, page 22.

Bouley, Jane, "What's in a street name?," *Branford Review*, July 26, 1995, page 3.

Carr, John C., *Old Branford*, Branford Tercentenary Committee, 1935, reprinted Branford Historical Society, 1985.

Estela, Kevin, *A History of the Development of Strategic Highways in Hartford, CT*, Hartford: Trinity College, 2003.

Fletcher, Richard H. and James M. West, *Along Branford Shore, A Delightful Trolley Ride*, Shore Line Trolley Museum.

Forty Years of Highway Development in Connecticut, 1895-1935, Tercentenary Commission State of Connecticut, Committee on Historical Publications, XLVI: New Haven: Yale University Press, 1935.

Hanna, Archibald, *A Brief History of the Thimble Islands in Branford, Connecticut*, Archon Books, 1970.

Jacobson, Wayne E., *Stony Creek Mapanscrap Book*, Stony Creek Church of Christ Congregational, North Haven: William Mack Co., 1982.

Kirby, John B., Jr., *A Brief History of Pawson Park from Early Times to 1916; Discord in Stony Creek 1892; Stony Creek in 1880, Its History, Natives, and Summer People; The Pine Orchard Shore, A Brief History* and a *Glimpse at the Summer of 1916*; privately printed, various dates.

Kurumi, Connecticut Roads, www.kurumi.com/roads/ct/index.html

McKenzie, Gertrude Farnham, *A Brief History of Stony Creek*, New Haven: Van Dyck & Co., 1933.

Miller, Herbert C., *The History of North Branford and Northford*, Derby: Bacon Printing Co., 1982.

Mitchell, Isabel S., *Roads and Road Making in Colonial Connecticut*, Tercentenary Commission State of Connecticut, Committee on Historical Publications, XIV: New Haven: Yale University Press, 1935.

Nash, Harriett Damon, *Early Settlement of Short Beach*, Branford Review, August 29, September 5, September 12, September 19, September 26, 1929.

Palm, Phyllis and Sally D'Amato, *Summer Island, A Century of History and Nostalgia*, Branford: Anchor Press, 2000.

Simonds, Sarah P., "Early days of Short Beach," *Branford Review*, October 10, October 17, October 24, October 31, November 14, November 21, November 27, 1929, January 30, 1930.

Weir, William L., "What's in a name?" *Branford Review*, July 26, 1993, page 3.

Young, A.M. Company Maps, Branford Historical Society archives.

ABOUT THE AUTHOR

Jane Peterson Bouley is the Branford, Connecticut Town Historian and has focused her research on primary material and resources with an emphasis on the nineteenth and twentieth centuries. She is the author or coauthor of *The Civil War Soldiers of Branford, Connecticut, Damascus Cemetery, Mill Plain Cemetery, Supply Pond*, and other works. She is a recipient of an Award of Merit from the Connecticut League of Historical Societies and was inducted into the Branford Education Hall of Fame in 1999.

www.ingramcontent.com/pod-product-compliance
Lightning Source LLC
Chambersburg PA
CBHW071904290426
44110CB00013B/1279